Praise for Jane Atkinsor

"If ever there was a right book at the right time, Jane's new book, *Scaling Your Speaking Business,* is it! Jane keeps you totally engaged, not just with invaluable ideas, but also with real-life examples, thought-provoking exercises, and questions that will lead you to action. Jane continues to deliver real value to speakers with this book. Get it today!"

Joe Calloway, Author, *The Leadership Mindset*

"*Scaling Your Speaking Business* is a must-read for anyone serious about earning an income with speaking. Jane's depth of knowledge around the speaking business is unparalleled, and I know I would not have achieved the significant growth in my business I now have without her. I'm confident that if you follow Jane's advice, your return on investment will be multiplied hundreds, or even thousands, of times over."

Pamela Barnum, M.P.A., J.D., Trust Strategist
and Nonverbal Communication Expert

"Until you scale, you don't have a business, you have a practice. Jane's book is a paint-by-numbers process to find those lucrative ways to scale your expertise into sustainable revenue!"

Vince Poscente, *New York Times* Bestselling
Author, Hall of Fame Speaker & Olympian

"No one understands the business of speaking like Jane Atkinson. If you're a speaker with a message worth sharing, you're doing yourself a disservice if you don't listen to everything she says. She is the one person who can truly show you how to scale your speaking business, doing what you love most and getting paid well doing it."

Lisa Larter, Author, *Pilot to Profit*

"Lots of authors make too-good-to-be-true claims like 'earn more by doing less,' but Jane over-delivers on the promise. *Scaling Your Speaking Business* is a *must-read* for any speaker looking to amplify their influence and income while simultaneously streamlining their business and simplifying their lives. Working with Jane has been a game-changer in my business and this book will be a game-changer for yours, too.

Brittany Hodak, International Keynote Speaker
and Chief Experience Officer, Experience.com

Scaling Your Speaking Business

10 STRATEGIES FOR EARNING MORE WHILE DOING LESS

JANE ATKINSON

ISBN 978-0-9917512-6-6 (Paperback)
ISBN 978-0-9917512-7-3 (e-Book)
ISBN 978-0-9917512-8-0 (Audio Book)

First Printing

Editor: Catherine Leek of Green Onion Publishing
Cover and Interior Design, Electronic Page Composition: Kim Monteforte of Kim Monteforte Graphic Design Services

Printed in Canada.

This book is dedicated to my team!

Sometimes when you're the one on stage, the players in the background don't get their full due. My team – I thank you. Without you, I'd be lost! We are small but mighty and each member is pivotal in helping my business grow.

Carolyn Cummey has brought systems and wisdom that would have taken me years to figure out on my own. You are like a sister to me.

Monica Martin brings kindness and the attention to detail that every business needs. She's my right arm and sometimes my left. And we have some great laughs!

Jen McDonough runs The Wealthy Speaker School and brings heart, compassion and knowledge to all of our students. Thank you for putting kindness first.

Theresa Scholes has brought knowledge and structure to my business and our courses and is so appreciated. She's been here since the beginning!

I dedicate this book to these amazing women!

Contents

STRATEGY #4

STRATEGY #5

STRATEGY #6

STRATEGY #7

Foreword

How exactly do you scale a speaking business? What does it take? Where do you even start? These were questions I had asked myself almost since the day I had started my business. I knew my ultimate goal was to scale, but rapid growth and a busy schedule kept getting in my way.

Let's make sure we are on the same page with understanding what I mean by growing my business versus scaling it. What is the difference? What are the benefits?

When your business is in growth mode, you increase revenue but you also increase the resources to achieve that revenue. Meaning you use a lot of what you earn to fund the continuous growth. So, why earn more if it is just going to cost you more?

Scaling, on the other hand, is about adding revenue faster and at a greater rate than you incur costs. You make more, spend less, and create more profit. You also build a business that is less dependent upon you for success and revenue generation – my true endgame for building my business.

That was my challenge. I understood my goal, but couldn't find the time and space to achieve it. Enter COVID-19.

The disruption that COVID-19 created, combined with my desire to scale, led me down a path of new initiatives, fresh opportunities and the freedom I dreamed of when starting my business. And that is what I wish for you as well, and what I know you will find in this innovative and much-needed new book Jane has put together.

For more than 20 years, professional speakers have been turning to Jane Atkinson for answers. In her first book, *The Wealthy Speaker, 2.0,* Jane revealed the roadmap for becoming a successful professional speaker.

Written from her personal experience and wisdom, as both a speaker agent and manager, Jane held back nothing in the pages and chapters. It was that book, and Jane Atkinson, that launched my speaking career.

Now, here we are in a new time, a new decade, and an entirely new marketplace. And while many are struggling to make the shift or figure out what to do, the best in the industry know it's time once again to turn to Jane Atkinson.

And Jane does not disappoint. *Scaling Your Speaking Business* is groundbreaking, innovative information every speaker needs to navigate this pace of change, and take their business to the next level.

In every chapter, Jane speaks from her own experience of how she transformed her personal business, and how she has coached some of the most successful speakers to make this same transition.

Get ready as you read through each chapter to be exposed to a different way of thinking, be challenged by new paradigms, and to be open-minded enough to make these shifts. You will laugh and you will learn as Jane reveals it all from setting higher goals, to creating multiple revenue streams to building a power-packed team.

She answers the question that most speakers today want answered – how do I work less and make more? In addition, she puts it all together in a read that is engaging, fun, and brimming with innovative ideas and easy-to-implement strategies.

I am excited for you to discover this book, and even more excited to watch as you scale your business and create the life and career you truly want.

Meridith Elliott Powell

Are You Ready to Scale?

Welcome to *Scaling Your Speaking Business*! This is going to be a fun ride! Are you ready?

Scaling for the Wealthy Speaker

As someone who has had a bird's-eye view of speakers and their growth over the past 30 plus years, I'm excited to share with you some of the things that I've learned along the way, not just in helping speakers scale (first, through my work as an agent selling speakers and for the past 15 years as a coach), but in my own business too.

Back in my early days as a member of Dan Sullivan's Strategic Coach® program, Dan posed a question to us. "What would it look like to multiply your business by ten?"

"Ten times my business! Are you crazy? That's not possible," I thought. But, then, after another year or so, I did some calculations and realized that I had already increased my business by a factor of ten. That was the moment that I realized there were no limits to what was possible.

> ***"While the difficult takes time, the impossible just takes a little longer."***
>
> ***Art Berg***

Now, I can hear some of you thinking. "Having my business grow ten times larger would mean a heck of a lot more work. How can I possibly take on that much more? Whether it's on the road speaking or managing what I have going on already, my bandwidth is already strained."

I get it. I thought that way too. However, over the 15-year history of owning my business, I have been studying what works – learning, adopting, testing, failing and succeeding. And the reason I'm writing this book is to show you what's possible for your business. You don't, in fact, have to work harder to enjoy a higher income! And I'm going to show you the ten strategies for doing just that!

Now, I have to tell you straight up – everything I know I have learned from either my mentors, Strategic Coach® (Dan Sullivan) and Self Coaching Scholars (Brooke Castillo), or my friends and colleagues in the speaking business at CAPS (Canadian Association of Professional Speakers) and NSA (National Speakers Association). I've also had the privilege of interviewing hundreds of successful speakers and business owners for The Wealthy Speaker Podcast, speakers who have generously shared best practices and have shown me and my listeners what's possible in this industry.

My ideas are a culmination of 30 years of watching what works and what doesn't inside our industry and, more importantly, from outside our industry. There's nothing I love more than sitting at a lunch between an innovative, multi-millionaire farmer and an app developer, learning from what they are doing and applying it to our business.

If you've had your head buried in speaking, there's no better time to pop up out of that paradigm and start thinking about your business as a *business*. One that can grow to whatever degree you choose! Whether your goal is to go from $100K to $250K or $250K to a million, scaling is all about growing your numbers. And more importantly creating a business that allows you the lifestyle and freedom that's perfect for you! Maybe even a business you can sell?

Note: If you're just getting started in the speaking business, I highly recommend that you read *The Wealthy Speaker 2.0* as well. It's a pre-cursor to delving into the concepts this book. You're going to want to get the foundations in place and get your business launched and running smoothly, before you scale. Does that make sense?

So if the sky's the limit, what's that look like?

Imagine the Perfect Day in Your Business!

Get comfortable for a minute and take a deep breath. Let's imagine that you're having the perfect day in your life as an expert who speaks, as a business owner.

You spend your day doing the things that you love. Perhaps it's speaking live or virtual, consulting, coaching or running your mastermind or online course. Possibly you're developing a new product or presentation. Or maybe you wake up, open your laptop and your in-box is full of new order notices that came in during the night. Income that will require no effort on your part!

Is this sounding good so far?

When you work with your clients, it fills you up, rather than draining you. You have weeded out the low paying work and feel terrific standing tall in your fees, knowing that you provide amazing value.

You travel as much, or as little, as you like. You deliver the types of programs that are perfect for you. It's business by design!

Your business is set up to run by itself, like a well-oiled machine. You have a strong team, all working within their strengths. The work that you do personally is high level – writing, selling, producing and delivering new ideas and content. Everything else goes to the team, for whom you are a strong leader.

You have a robust funnel, which means that a continuous flow of business comes to you, and you have strong partnerships that bring in additional revenue. Business feels easy.

You work hours that are perfect for you. You are able to take true vacations where you check out completely and rejuvenate your mind, body and spirit. Your family loves how much time you spend with them and, of course, benefits from the security and perks of the wealth that you've created.

Not only have you learned how to make money at far beyond average volumes, you have learned how to keep money and have rainy day accounts tucked away for emergencies and special projects.

The goal is to build the business that is perfect for you!

This business brings you freedom. Freedom to work as much or as little as you want. Freedom to give back to charities that are near and dear to your heart. Freedom to live the life of your dreams with your family.

Does the vision sound good?

This isn't a pipe dream. This is the benefit of scaling your business. And this is exactly what we are going to share with you throughout this book.

Remember, this is *your* vision for *your* business and you can take or leave any of the pieces and add your own.

It's not one size fits all. Create your own perfect day by trying Exercise 1 (also available on your Bonus Page).

BONUS PAGE

Exercise 1: The Perfect Day in Your Life:
www.speakerlauncher.com/scale

Note: If you've done this exercise after reading *The Wealthy Speaker 2.0* or as a student of The Wealthy Speaker School, and more than six months have passed, be sure to revisit it. Our goals and ideas are constantly changing and this may be an opportunity to get even clearer on your vision for your future.

Exercise 1:
THE PERFECT DAY IN YOUR LIFE

Imagine you're having the perfect day in your life five years from now. What does that look like? Who's around you? Where do you travel? How often do you speak (live or virtual)? At what fee? What other sources of revenue do you have? What do you do in your free time?

Now that you've done your first piece of homework, keep the "The Perfect Day in Your Life" handy for review on a regular basis. Your brain will love this vision and will help you develop ideas to make it come true. And use the master Scaling Checklist (coming up next) as your implementation strategy for making this happen.

One thing at a time.

Before we dive into scaling your speaking business, I'd like to cover a couple of the assumptions that we'll be making about you.

Your Foundations

One assumption is that you consider yourself an "expert" not a speaker. We talk a lot more about this in *The Wealthy Speaker 2.0*, but the basic premise is that speaking is just one of the ways that you distribute your knowledge. Your expertise can be delivered in multiple ways – and we're going to be exploring many of those delivery systems in this book.

Another assumption is that you have your foundations already in place. You have your business up and running – perhaps you followed the "ready, aim, fire" process that we mapped out for you in *The Wealthy Speaker 2.0*. If you haven't got the basics in place, then you may want to circle back and read that book before diving into this one.

Think about it like this.

The foundation of your business (your website, your marketing, your sales and gig management processes) are all part of the foundation of the house. It's the concrete and the floors. Scaling is like adding a second floor to that house. Without the foundation or the first floor, it will crumble. Does this make sense?

Now as far as having your "house" in order, we're going to give you a series of things to have in place before you scale, but let's just make sure that your business is up and running and solid *before* you try to race ahead to that seven-figure income level.

The Scaling Checklist

You've mapped out the perfect day in your life. Now, let's see where we're starting from. We'll be returning to Exercise 1 as well as checking items off Your Scaling Checklist (see Exercise 2) throughout the book to make sure that you are making progress.

You might take a look at the list in Exercise 2 and think, "Yikes, no! I'm not ready!" And if that's the case, don't worry. We all have to start somewhere.

Your scaling journey may take months or, if you are anything like me, it may take years. Being in a hurry likely will not help make things go faster. As you can see by the quiz, there are a lot of moving parts to scaling. Take each chunk one at a time. Rome wasn't built in a day. And many people who have scaled their businesses took many years to get there.

Let's do this on your timeline!

Are you ready to scale? Take the quiz on the next page!

You'll want to circle back to this quiz often in order to check off boxes as you go, so be sure to highlight or bookmark this page. We've also included it on your Bonus Page.

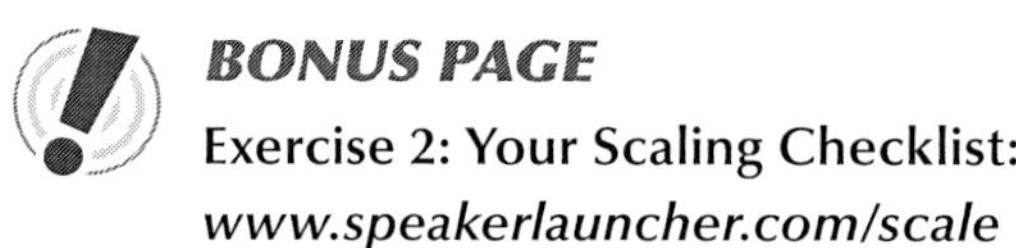

BONUS PAGE

Exercise 2: Your Scaling Checklist:
www.speakerlauncher.com/scale

Exercise 2:
YOUR SCALING CHECKLIST

Let's check in and see where you are in the scaling process, see if there is work to be done. Don't stress if you can't check many of these boxes yet, this is just the beginning!

Yes	No	
☐	☐	You have lofty goals set out for yourself.
☐	☐	All of your ducks are aligned (money, mindset, team, business model) and you are ready for growth.
☐	☐	You are prepared to invest financially in your business.
☐	☐	The systems you have in place keep everything running like a well-oiled machine.
☐	☐	Your business offers only the revenue streams that you love.
☐	☐	You make money while you sleep (passive income).
☐	☐	You've dropped your low paycheck activities.
☐	☐	The funnel is in place (and working) to bring new business to your door consistently.
☐	☐	You have partners in place who sell your work.
☐	☐	You're excellent at making money as well as keeping money (your financial house is in order).

Homework, Worksheets & Bonuses

There are a couple of ways for you to do the exercises in this book.

If you have the paperback version, the exercises and thought-provoking questions are here with space for you to complete them. There's nothing I love more than to see a book all marked up with Post-it® Notes, highlighter and writing.

Another option is to go to the Bonus Page I've set up for you on my site: www.speakerlauncher.com/scale. You can download all of the exercises, worksheets and questions and keep them in a separate binder, ready to use as you go through *Scaling Your Speaking Business.*

Throughout the book you'll see references to the Bonus Page. You're not going to want to miss out on all of the links and videos we provide, so be sure you check it out at some point.

Once you sign up, you'll receive a link in your in-box. Be sure to bookmark the page to refer to again and again.

• • •

Scaling is not the solution to poor cash flow or a lack of business income. Scaling is only a possibility when we have all of our ducks in a row.

Basically, the only thing you need to get started is an openness to learn and a willingness to invest. Investing your time and money is essential. If you are short on either, I hope you will take the steps to rectify before diving in.

And when it comes to growing your business, we'll work on your mindset around investing in yourself and your business in Strategy #1, under "As If" Thinking.

Thought-Provoking Questions

Are you ready to scale?

What makes you feel confident when it comes to growing your business?

Let's go on this journey together and explore the possibilities, shall we?

Strategy #1

Aim Higher with Your Goals

I was trying to think of whose story would be a perfect example to show you what's possible. Well, duh, I realized that it's my own. I never set out to be an example of what's possible but I will gladly take that role in your life if you'll allow it. And, yes, I'll be sharing lots of speaker examples with you that will inspire you to go big in your business, but my own story really is worthy of noting.

Success Story #1: Jane!

When I got into the speaking business it wasn't, and never has been, to put myself on the stage.

I was working as a waitress and bartender at my local pub, making pretty good tips and living with my parents after returning from a year in Australia. At 25 years old, I had an education in data processing (computer programming) but really didn't fit the mold for that profession. I had a lot of "temp" jobs during the day, which was a terrific way to learn about business. I'd worked for an airline, a radio station and a big six accounting firm, just to name a few. I was a sponge so I absorbed something from every job posting sometimes staying more than a year for a maternity leave. (In Canada we have up to 18 months maternity leave – nice, hey?)

I was coming to the end of a contract with 3M in their personal products department (the people who make Post-it® Notes and all kinds of other cool things) and I watched a Les Brown special on PBS called "Live Your Dreams." It hit me like a ton of bricks, "I know what I want to do for a profession!" After many years of wandering, I declared, "I want to work for a motivational speaker!!" Poof, out it went to the universe.

Helping Others Succeed

The next day I told one of my colleagues at 3M my idea, and she said, "My best friend just left her VP position here to pursue her dream of becoming a motivational speaker!" Bing, bang, boom, I have my first job as "marketing director" for a motivational speaker. (I hit the jackpot with Betska K-Burr, a leadership expert who really taught me the ropes.)

And, so, I learned.

Three years. Straight commission. Basement office. Paying my dues.

We doubled Betska's business three years in a row. And people started to take notice. I was recruited into another job; this one bigger and better and out in Vancouver. I went from living with my parents to renting a beautiful high-rise apartment overlooking a golf course. At work, my corner office was beside the big boss, Peter Legge, who is a publishing magnate and multi-millionaire. (He spoke on the side and it was my job to book him more business.) And once again, I learned. I absorbed. I upgraded my skills and knowledge. Only this time I got to see what happens in a 20-million-dollar company. Meanwhile, we increased Peter's speaking business year over year.

That's when I started getting even more attention as a rock star in speaking marketing.

So, then a third opportunity presented itself, one that would take my skills south of the border, which is exciting for a Canadian. I moved to Dallas to work for Olympic athlete Vince Poscente. And it just so happened that Vince's wife owned a speakers bureau.

We started in a shabby little office with five people and a dog – three on the bureau side, and Vince and myself on the other. I sat in on every meeting for the speakers bureau for six years and I watched as we grew from a staff of 5 to 25. We went from that crappy little office to a funky brick building downtown. We grew Vince's business exponentially over four years, and it went to seven figures as a result. In my final two years in Dallas, I ran the exclusives division of the speakers bureau. But after six years state side, and post 9-11, it was time for me to go. I had learned in Texas what "big" really meant.

Now a footnote about that speakers bureau. I watched it grow quickly and I had a bird's-eye view as its leadership shifted and changed. Several years after I left, that business went bankrupt, taking a lot of speakers' fees with it. The lesson for me was that when it comes to scaling your own business have patience (take your time), be a strong leader with a clear vision, and always, always, watch your cash flow.

While living in Dallas, I had a life coach (shout out to Rich Fettke who resided in California) who helped me see what my future might look like. Single at the time, it was very hard to see exactly what I wanted in the distance but my coach took me there. And the life I lead today is exactly what we mapped out.

When I returned to Canada, with 15 years under my belt in the business, I hung out my shingle as a coach. People had been asking me all along, "How did you make Betska/Peter/Vince so successful?" And I knew I had the skills to help them. I trained as a coach (CTI – Coaches Training Institute) and proceeded to grow my business.

My Success Journey

Over the next 15 years, I wrote four books, including bestseller *The Wealthy Speaker 2.0*, helped thousands of speakers grow their businesses (some beyond their wildest dreams), created a school (The Wealthy Speaker School) and developed live events and masterminds (Inner Circle Mastermind) for speakers who wanted to scale. And in the fall of

2020, I started certification in a Mindset Coaching model designed to help my clients blow past barriers to big time success.

So that sounds like success, but is it?

That's not the whole story.

Moving back to Canada to be closer to my aging parents was a huge step for me. I'd had wanderlust for over a decade and I was now ready to plant some roots. I bought a small condo and set about finding my perfect man. I did it with the same strategy I had applied to business. (You can read about this in an "off brand" book I wrote called *The Frog Whisperer* – available only on Kindle.) I really worked on myself to get ready, and when I was truly ready, John appeared. By the time he entered the picture, I already had a very successful coaching practice, had written a book, and owned the condo as well as a tiny vacation property.

John's business as an electrical contractor has him busy at times, but it also affords us a lot of vacation time. Getting him to retire has been my goal for a while, so that we can be mobile. Over the 13+ years we've been together, we've purchased four homes. My brother, who has cerebral palsy, lives in one of the houses, which we renovated for his wheelchair. My mom and I are partners on her condo, a stone's throw from our primary house. Our most recent acquisition is our vacation home on the lake, which we've doubled in value with a massive renovation. This is the tranquil place I wrote the majority of this book.

I tell you this because way back in Dallas, my coach Rich and I dreamed up this property and the times I would have with family here. I'm a step-mom and g-ma. We have six amazing grandkids (ages 1 to 13) and having them grow up on this lake, learning how to water ski, is the best gift ever.

When my coach and I started to put this vision together, I couldn't even imagine not being single, let alone being a gramma. I couldn't imagine not worrying about money. And I certainly couldn't imagine having a bank account healthy enough that it would sustain me and my team through the worst months in my business's 15-year history when a pandemic hit the world.

Today, I can imagine so much more – and I'm truly just getting started!

I can't wait to have you dive into the Possibility Expander (found later in this Strategy). It will allow you to go beyond what's been possible so far in your life.

To have started as a waitress and a "temp" to sitting at the lake, watching the hummingbird play, and a kayaker glide by while working on my fifth book seems pretty crazy to me. Of course, the road has had bumps, losses, sorrow and failure.

Moving beyond your wildest dreams in your business, means risking failure. You're going to try things, and they will stink up the place. But guess what? You'll try something else and success will smell sweet. And when your personal life requires your attention due to illness, divorce, family or kid drama, you'll have the systems, team, freedom and flexibility to do what you need to do.

I don't need to tell you this. You already know this, because you've been through success, failure, loss and drama before.

If you're not willing to fail, you're not ready to scale.

Don't let those stop you.

Now is the time to step up to exactly what you want in this next 2.0 version of your business.

The Wealthy Speaker Mindset

I bring this mindset concept forward from *The Wealthy Speaker 2.0* because it's such a significant piece of the scaling puzzle. And, bonus for you, my own mindset work has evolved since I wrote that book. I used to think that mindset was a portion of your success, a percentage. Now, I believe your mindset is 100% responsible for your results.

Let me say that again.

What you think about most of the time is 100% responsible for your actions and hence your results. Mindset is imperative to scaling, and if you don't have your mindset – your thoughts about your business – in hand, this will be the first thing to work on.

SUCCESS STORY

Jason Harris

Aiming as High as the Sky

Jason had grown up in a setting where his life could have gone in many directions. With a single mom raising six kids in East Oakland, California, the odds for high achievement were not stacked in his favor.

Growing up he witnessed family members and other young people from his community involved in illicit activities and he made many decisions throughout his youth that would alter his destiny.

After being expelled from regular school and sent to an alternative school – not once, but twice – Jason decided focus was required during his high school years. His determination to graduate high school and attend college were life changing and enabled Jason to be the first in his family to go to college.

And he didn't go to just any college. Jason attended one of the most competitive colleges in the country, the US Air Force Academy. After four grueling years, Jason graduated, earning a coveted slot to attend pilot training. After finishing the year-long, fast-paced training program and earning his wings, Jason was assigned to fly the C-130 Hercules. Throughout his military career Jason has flown various aircraft, led missions and escorted people all around the world.

Jason entered into professional speaking after experiencing life as a military officer and pilot along with becoming an airline pilot. He realized that he could provide a transformational message to corporate and association audiences based on his unique experiences. He chose to aim high and appeared on the speaking scene at a high level.

Are you aiming high enough in your life?

At one time in his life, Jason couldn't imagine the life that he lives today. I hope it will inspire you to aim high as well!

Thought-Provoking Questions

So what are your thoughts about how high you can go?

___

___

___

What might get in the way of your goals? And what will you do about it?

___

___

___

I hope that you aren't limiting yourself. And to make sure that you aren't, check out the next exercise called "The Possibility Expander."

Going Beyond Your Wildest

For this exercise, you'll need to suspend any and all disbelief about whether or not you can achieve your goals. Really get into an "anything is possible" head space. Come in with an "I'll believe it when I see it" mindset, and you'll be doing yourself a disservice.

You heard my story of building my business over the last 15 years, but let me share with you something more recent.

In March 2020 all speaking engagements were effectively wiped off our collective industry calendar. Many were postponed until later dates, some canceled all together. I don't have to tell you, you lived it.

My initial thought was, "Oh my goodness, my industry has been wiped out!" I was in shock and the feeling that immediately followed was fear. I went into a tailspin that lasted several days. I even entertained the idea of selling our house and downsizing. Some of you went this direction, and some of you did the opposite.

Looking back now (with the assistance of an exercise created by Dan Sullivan) I realize my default position in a time of crisis isn't always one of confidence. If I were to rate it on a scale of 1 to 10, with 10 being most confident, I have to say I started at 4 and worked my way towards 8. In hindsight, I recognize that my goal now is to land at 8, if not immediately, then more quickly.

Once I identified the horrible thought that was floating through my brain – my industry is wiped out – I took steps to change it.

I started to think about all of the speakers who would need my counsel. I was asked to participate in several "state of the industry" webinars, one in Canada, one for North America and one global. I did a four-week "Brand Camp" series with a great friend, Chris West. All of these events were initiated by others, and I was invited to participate.

I quickly realized that people needed me. I knew that I was the voice of reason for many speakers and I could not withdraw. It took a while, but I slowly built back my mojo.

It was at that time that Brooke Castillo (who leads The Life Coach School to which I belong) asked us to set an "impossible goal," and to keep the time frame short. So, despite being in the middle of the worst month in my company's history (March 2020), I set an impossible goal to earn $50,000 in April and May. That would allow me to keep the entire team in place, and pay my bills with some left over. The deadline was May 31.

Most importantly, my new thought about what was happening all around me was "speakers need me now more than ever."

I've told people since then that it was like flipping a light switch. Speakers came flocking to my School, and to me for private coaching. We made our goal by April 30, an entire month before deadline! I was thrilled.

It's with that idea of "impossible" in mind that I want you to approach Exercise 3: The Possibility Expander – and remember you can find all the exercises on your Bonus Page. When I set my $50K goal, I didn't know *how* it was going to happen, I just chose a number that felt impossible.

BONUS PAGE

Exercise 3: The Possibility Expander:

www.speakerlauncher.com/scale

When you do this exercise don't get caught up in the how. Just go for it.

Exercise 3:

THE POSSIBILITY EXPANDER

If you had no limits on your business, no limits on what was possible, what would your annual revenue goal be? I'd suggest that you give yourself a year or more to get there. (There's going to be work to do as you work through our 10 strategies.)

Year: ____________ Financial Goal: $______________________

How would it feel to earn this much?

> **Examples:** *It will feel fabulous; I'll feel proud of myself; it will feel very much the same as my current income level but the level of security for me and my family will have improved greatly.*

____

____

____

What will change if your business produces this revenue?

> **Examples:** *Freedom from financial worries; less responsibility; more team members in place; more expensive problems; more leading less doing.*

Note, there are problems that come with running a larger organization. If you go from one team member to five, be realistic that it's not all rainbows and sunshine. Our goal here is to prepare you.

____

____

____

What won't change if your business produces this revenue?

> **Examples:** *I'll still have problems; who I am won't change; what I value and how much I work won't change.*

____

____

____

How hard will you work to build this revenue?

> **Examples:** *My work habits will stay the same; I'll work less because I'll have more freedom and a strong team.*

____

____

____

What have you achieved in your business in the past that gives you confidence in reaching this goal?

> **Examples:** *Written books; know how to make – and keep – money; I have already grown my business by a factor of ten.*

____

____

____

Great job! Did you expand your possibilities?

I remember a conversation with Annie, a member of my Inner Circle Mastermind. During COVID-19 in early 2020, Annie had been working from dawn till dusk, hustling like I've never seen anyone hustle. At the beginning, she was so nervous about not having enough to pay the bills (a story deeply rooted in her childhood with a highly dysfunctional family and never having enough to eat) that she was willing to work for any fee.

During our coaching session, I reminded Annie of the value that she brought to the table. She told me later that she hung up from me and almost immediately booked her highest fee virtual event ever! That light switch had flipped for Annie and once she remembered her value, she was able to stand tall in her fees.

For Annie and other speakers, the pandemic dragged on and on making it necessary to circle back to mindset work again and again, in order to maintain your ability to stand tall. And it's certainly not work that is over for me, I do this on a daily basis.

SUCCESS STORY
Chris West

Holding Out for the Dream

One of my good friends and colleagues, Chris, is an expert in speaker demo videos, but his business goes far beyond that. I know when I start coaching one of Chris's clients that they will have their marketing and message down cold and their materials will be of the highest quality. Because Chris is a quality individual.

Over the course of Chris's 10 years in business, as he grew, his family and kids were also growing. He and his wife Chelsea had decided to hold off on buying a home until it could be their dream property – a place with plenty of room to spread out where they could run their business, but also work with disadvantaged kids.

Over the years they were tempted to purchase as nearly perfect conditions presented. All of their friends were building in a community where they would have fit in perfectly, but it just wasn't the dream. So they held out. The vision for the house and land was coming to Chris during meditations; he would know it when he saw it.

And then one day, it happened!

They drove by the dream. A home on an acreage that was perfect for what they had envisioned. It had just gone on the market and the realtor had already fielded hundreds of calls about this property! They were taking all of the offers to the homeowner in ten days. They knew their offer would have to be great! They had to move quickly to get an entire year of taxes done on time to be able to put together the financing and a strong offer.

They put in an amazing bid (complete with video apropos of Chris) and it was down to them and one other offer for a lot more money. And they got rejected. They lost the house to the higher bidder. For a week, they struggled to deal with that blow, but then something happened.

The original deal fell through and after a month of ups and downs, financing and inspections, challenges that would make most people throw in the towel, they got the property of their dreams.

Chris and Chelsea didn't compromise on the dream. Nor did they get distracted. They faced hurdle after hurdle, setback after setback, and they made it work.

Thought-Provoking Questions

Is your dream worth holding onto?

____

____

____

How far will you go to make it happen?

____

____

____

The Wealthy Speaker Meditation

Now I know I'm preaching to the choir when I say that what you consume in terms of reading and entertainment is going to reflect your thoughts and your results. I'm a bit of a news junky so the pandemic challenged my mindset for months on end. I'm much more invested in politics, especially US politics, than I want to be, but it affects my business and I want to stay current on what my clients are facing with the economy. (Year over year I've run about 70-80% US-based clients.)

Every once in a while, I do a news detox – several days or a week with no news. It's hard due to my need to be "in the know," but you'd be surprised at how little you miss in a week. During the detox, I'm conscious to only substitute with positive things. I listen to podcasts that lift me up, explore new meditations on YouTube and try to work some yoga into the mix. You know what they say "garbage in, garbage out."

My favorite go-to meditation for being uplifted is The Wealthy Speaker Meditation. When I need something positive to shift my thoughts, I reach for this easy ten-minute guided meditation. You'll find the meditation on your Bonus Page.

BONUS PAGE

The Wealthy Speaker Meditation: *Speakerlauncher.com/scale*

If you're feeling down about your revenue for the month, listen to this meditation every morning for a week. Some clients and students even do it for 30 days straight to really lock in the message. Listening to something positive about money can only help. It doesn't have to be this meditation, but anything that calms your mind will be a step in the right direction.

The Thought Model

Someday I may write a book on the Wealthy Speaker Mindset because I believe in it so much. Until that materializes I want to share this Thought Model with you that I learned from Brooke Castillo. You might scoff at the idea of "thought work" but I've watched Brooke's business scale, from $1 million to $10 million and, at the time of this printing, $35 million. I've learned from her mistakes (and there have been a few along the way) and I've learned from her teaching. If you'd like to follow her work, check out Brooke's podcast called "The Life Coach School Podcast."

It is called the Thought Model – perhaps you've heard of it, or have already used something like it. I like the way Brooke uses it.

In fact, I'm so excited to become proficient at teaching this model to my clients that I'm doing a year-long certification in the method. Why would I need something like this after coaching for 15 years and over 10,000 hours already? Because it makes my clients unstoppable. If we can manage their thoughts – the sky is the limit.

Here's the breakdown:

C = Circumstances
T = Thoughts
F = Feelings
A = Actions
R = Results

- **Circumstances.** Are the things that happen in the world around us – things that we don't control. They are factual. Examples include the weather, our pasts, other people's behavior, the economy, global crises. We treat circumstances as neutral because we cannot change them.
- **Thoughts.** Are the sentences that constantly run through our minds. Sometimes we are aware of our thoughts, but often we aren't. Examples include, "I'm not scaling fast enough," "I'll never get there," "My client will never pay that much." You see how powerful it might be to change our thoughts? We can't change circumstances, but we can change our thoughts about the circumstances.
- **Feelings.** Are the emotions we feel in our bodies and they're directly related to the thoughts we are thinking. Examples include dejection, sadness, pride, excitement. Emotions are voluntary because we can change what we feel by changing our thoughts.
- **Actions.** Refer to behaviors, reactions or inaction. They are directly related to our feelings. An example might be you think clients don't have any money to pay you, so you don't pick up the phone to ask. Or you are pretty sure you lost the engagement, so you don't follow up at the arranged time.
- **Results.** Are the effects of our actions. Examples include having a zero-revenue month because you had the thought that "everybody's on vacation in August, why bother?" Choosing different actions will lead us to different results.

The Thought Model is a logical way to take a look at how your thoughts are impacting your results.

For instance, you might think, "Someone must be booking business in August and nobody else is calling." The feeling that comes from that might be determination. The action becomes you sending out 50 e-mails to prospective clients, maybe with a joke about it being August or have they had their holiday. And perhaps the result? You find someone who is booking for the fall.

Let's run that scenario through the Thought Model (see Figure 1). Our goal is to move from an unintentional model (thought) to an intentional one.

FIGURE 1: ***The Thought Model Example***

Before – Unintentional	**After – Intentional**
Circumstance: It's August	Circumstance: It's August
Thought: Everybody's on vacation	Thought: Someone's got to be working!
Feeling: Defeated, delayed	Feeling: Determined
Action: Do nothing	Action: Send 50 e-mails
Result: $0	Result: Revenue booked

This book is about scaling, so I won't go into massive depth teaching you this model, but I want to reinforce these ideas.

- Circumstances may happen, but your thoughts about them are optional.
- You can start from the Results you want and work backwards. For instance, "What thought do I need to have in order to earn $1,000,000 in revenue in 20XX?"
- Check in on your thoughts prior to hopping on a client negotiation. Are you prepared to stand tall in your value and your fees?
- When you've had a difficult month financially, circle back and ask, "What was my thought this month?" It might surprise you.
- If needed, dust off some of your old books about thinking, such as *The Power of Positive Thinking* by Norman Vince Peale, *Think and Grow Rich* by Napoleon Hill and the more recent *Mindset* by Carol Dweck.

The Struggle Bus

The students in The Wealthy Speaker School often fall into one of two categories. One of struggle or one of determination. Now, of course, everyone goes through challenging times, but I've come to realize that it's difficult to change someone's mindset without a lot of work. If they are a struggler, I may have my work cut out for me.

Every time I hop on a call with Meridith, I know that she won't be riding the struggle bus. Here's her story.

SUCCESS STORY

Meridith Elliott Powell

Confidence at a Ten

Like so many speakers, 2020 started off strong for Meridith. By the end of February, she was looking at not only her best quarter ever, but probably her best year since becoming a speaker. Then in one week, the week of March 9th, everything changed.

In a matter of days, not only did all of her revenue disappear, but her business model (keynote speaking) became unworkable. Due to the global virus, she could no longer get on planes, travel round the world or engage with thousands of people.

At first, like many of us, she panicked. Unsure of what she was going to do to generate revenue she started to scramble for any idea she could think of – from selling her belongings on EBay to delivering pizzas! She considered everything. Her panic gave way to anger. Feeling like a victim, Meridith felt like this crisis was happening to her, and it was incredibly unfair.

Finally, her anger led to action. Not sure what to do or what action to take, Meridith turned to the only thing she could think of. Stop thinking about your own problems, and start focusing on your customers.

This entire transition took about a week. "I moved fast, thank goodness, from fear to anger to action," Meridith shared.

Understanding her customers would need help, Meridith declared herself an essential worker and started reaching out and checking-in with her customers. Making countless calls every day, she simply listened to how her customers were doing, the challenges they were facing and paid close attention to what they needed most in order to hold on through the crisis.

Asking simple questions like:

- How are things going?
- What are the biggest challenges you're facing?
- How is this crisis impacting you, your customers?
- What changes are happening in your industry?
- What is the biggest obstacle in your way right now?

The key was that the focus was 100% on the client and what they were going through. "I really believed I could be of service, and wanted to find a way to help. I guess you could say I ran into the fire, brought my hose, and was looking for the biggest flames to put out," she added.

The response was unbelievable! Not only were clients willing to talk, they were grateful to have someone listen. Conversation after conversation she was able to find out where her clients' biggest pain points were, how they were managing the challenges and what they most needed (that they did not have) to solve their problems.

"The conversations lead to the reinvention of my business model. I reached out to help my clients, but honestly they wound up helping me," Meridith recounted.

By talking and engaging clients, Meridith not only secured current relationships and increased client loyalty, but she found new business – a lot of new business. She created new products and services to solve her clients' problems, and she uncovered new opportunity after new opportunity.

"Just through having conversations, I would have clients say they were so glad I called. That they had been thinking about bringing someone in to speak to their team, or they knew of someone that I should talk with that needed my expertise. I never expected that simply caring about clients could lead to so much opportunity."

Within six months of losing all the business on her 2020 calendar, Meridith had turned her business completely around. Meridith's mindset and thoughts drove her into positive action, she shored up her confidence and she saw the results in her bottom line. In the end, 2020 turned out to be her best year on record – crisis and all!

Hopping Off the Bus

How would you know if you have the struggle mindset?

Well, here are some signs.

1. You feel powerless, unable to cope effectively with a problem.
2. You constantly focus on what's not working.
3. You struggle to make decisions and get stuck.
4. You lack confidence in your expertise and value.
5. You forget to celebrate the successes and focus only on the distance you are from your goal.
6. Deep down, you don't believe that you can have everything that you want.
7. You allow your past to dictate your future.

Making the decision to stop your cycle of struggle and move towards what you want may take some work, but it will begin with that decision.

Having been raised with the adage, "money doesn't grow on trees," I believed you had to work really, really hard to make a lot of money. Is that my belief now? Heck no! I believe you can work however hard you desire *and* have everything you want. It took me a few years to recondition my brain for this, but now I know it is possible and I know you can do this!

"As If" Thinking

What does it mean to make decisions from a place where you have already achieved your goals?

Can we agree that setting and writing down goals is powerful? The beauty of the brain is that, when we set a goal, it takes in the idea, allows it to germinate and then starts to work subconsciously on finding the path to that goal.

But what if we also lived, and made decisions, from that place where our goals have already come into fruition? What if we made our decisions *as if* they were true? Exercise 4 will help get you in that mindset.

Exercise 4: MAKING "AS IF" DECISIONS

Think about your income goal for next year (or the future).

Have you got a number in your head? (You wrote it down earlier in Exercise 3, The Possibility Expander.)

____

What if you made all of your decisions *as if* that number was already true?

____

____

____

Would that allow you the freedom to invest in your business with growth in mind?

____

____

____

Let's say your goal is to earn a million dollars. Every time a decision had to be made, you'd ask yourself, "What would a seven-figure business owner do?"

____

____

____

When we were getting The Wealthy Speaker School ready to launch, some tough decisions had to be made. We were going to be spending more than ever on team and on infrastructure.

Although it wasn't the cheapest learning platform, we chose LearnDash to house the lessons. We were hopeful that we were getting the best (stay tuned for an update on that). And we spent money to create a community that was easy for our students to participate in. Our team costs were in the thousands when it came to building the lessons and all of the worksheets and tools that went with them. We added a calendar format that our students could click on to place a School Class Call and all of the details right into their own calendars. All the fun and convenient features were just that – fun and convenient for our students – but all cost money to set up. In order to invest this way, I had to be thinking *as if* we had already reached our financial goal.

> ***What I do know for sure is that it's very hard to reach your goal with one foot on the gas pedal and one foot on the brake.***

Thought-Provoking Question

How close are you to operating in "as if" thinking?

____

____

____

If you have work to do on your goals, mindset, struggle or "as if" thinking, then this is the time to stop and reflect before moving into the next phase of your scaling, which is getting your foundation in place.

When we were discussing "as if" thinking, my friend and Business Strategist, Lisa Larter, said this:

> Wayne Gretzky has a quote, "skate to where the puck is going." The same is true in business. Hire and market for where you are going, not where you are right now. It's scary to invest resources into where you're headed but it's necessary if you want to get there without dropping balls or burning yourself out.

Always Be Learning

In the fall of 2020, our company suffered a "brute force attack" – a breach in security that caused hundreds of e-mails to go out to our clients, a small group of them receiving over a hundred of the same e-mail from us. Trying to work with LearnDash support to resolve this problem was slow and painful.

So, we made the difficult decision to move our entire School over to a different learning platform. A lesson in security – don't wait for something to go wrong to test your systems for security.

You might think I was upset about making a mistake on the learning platform. But guess what? Being willing to make mistakes is a part of the scaling process, it's a part of business.

Strategy #2

Do the Ground Work for Scaling

You might think that you are all set and ready to scale, but we need to check in on some things to ensure you have everything in place.

You know how you feel when you have a ton of clutter, but it's all hidden underneath your bed or in a closet. The clutter is still there. In the back of your mind. It's haunting you. And it's taking up mental space.

The ground work for scaling involves getting your house in order so that you can scale.

Getting Your House in Order

My own business has been forced to do this, which in turn has slowed down our efforts to scale. Each time an issue occurs, I think, "Well, we need to have this under control before we grow, or we'll have chaos on our hands." For example, at The Wealthy Speaker School we recognized that people who weren't engaged with us inside the School – the lurkers – had no loyalty to us; they were unlikely to become long-term clients, which is what we wanted. We needed to fix our engagement before we could scale.

There are four main areas of your business that need to be in place and under control prior to scaling, here's our checklist.

1. **Finances:** Do you have your financial house in order? Or do you have a lot of debt and dysfunction when it comes to your finances? Having your house in order means that you are in control of your money, it's not in control of you. I have clients and friends who like to bury their heads in the sand when it comes to looking at anything related to money. Is that you? If so, you're going to need to change your ways and ensure that you are seeing your P&L on a regular basis in order to grow.

2. **Team:** Do you have the right players in place to scale? Are you a perfectionist or a control freak? If you are still doing all of the jobs, even the $20/hour jobs yourself, then "Houston, we have a problem!" If you don't have a team, then scaling means that you are simply going to be working *x* times harder in order to earn *x* times more. We'll talk more about team when we get to Strategy #5.

3. **Time:** The same way that you want to be in control of your financial house, you always want to be in control of your time. Is your business running you, or are you running it? Typically if someone isn't in control of their time it means that they don't have a quality team in place who they trust to get the job done.

   "But, but, but," I can hear you saying. "What if I lose out on a speaking engagement because I'm on vacation?" Either you have someone on your team who can close a deal without you (ideal) or you agree ahead of time when and how you will check in. If you are on your phone 24/7, you have no boundaries on your time and scaling will be doable, but *exhausting* for you. That's not the goal! Having people and systems that you trust is essential to growth.

   Every once in a while I've had a client "no show" because something came up. They were "too busy" to work on their business. We'll talk a lot more about time later, but if you are "too busy" to stop and work on your business, you have some serious work to do within this strategy before proceeding to Strategy #3.

4. **Systems:** Now we're going to have an entire section on systems in Strategy #3, so I won't go into these deeply, but know that

you'll want to have a process for everything. Any e-mail that you send more than once should be a template. Any proposal you might repeat should have a master. Your CRM (Customer Relationship Management) should be working smoothly and collecting data that you can use and search. Your before-during-and-after presentation processes should be smooth, especially the collection of money and referrals. And most importantly, your funnel must be in place to bring business to your door. Systems is typically the area that most people need to work on prior to scaling their business and we'll help you go deep into each area in order to get ready.

Being in a big rush to scale may not serve you.

Have patience and get your pieces of the puzzle in place prior to growth and you'll ensure yourself the best shot at reaching your goal.

SUCCESS STORY

Neen James

Ready to Scale

When I wrapped up work with one of my former clients, Neen, she had strong foundations in place for scaling. She had been earning an above-average income for several years in both speaking and consulting and had decided as part of her next chapter to move her business to the sunny south. Neen moved into her waterfront home in Florida and proceeded to focus on systemizing everything to an even greater level.

She expanded her virtual team to help support her financial and lifestyle goals, including: a world-class personal trainer to focus on fitness, nutrition, and energy; a renowned marketing brain to design and automate e-mail marketing and product development; a social media strategist to increase engagement; a sales goddess for outbound outreach and sales conversations; and an advisory board to assist with strategic decisions.

> Her finances were in great shape and she was very much in control of her schedule, understanding the importance of downtime and self-care after years of being a road warrior.
>
> Neen's systems for bringing in and administering business were solid. She had everything set up on her phone so that she could do business from anywhere (literally an airport, another country, or even the boat). Her clients love her efficiency in getting them anything they require at any stage of a speaking or consulting engagement. Everything is organized, systemized and set up for ease of use.

With all of these systems and processes, team and finances in place, Neen is set to go as far as her heart desires when it comes to scaling her business.

Who Is Your Scaling Mentor?

When it comes to taking your business from $100K to $500K or from a half million to a million, someone who has gained the knowledge and experience in going before you should be in your corner.

Of course, it would be silly if I didn't make you aware that the majority of my private coaching and mastermind clients are in the throes of scaling. So if you would indeed like help, just write to me (jane@speakerlauncher.com) and we'll set up a chat.

A lot of people would like to find someone to mentor them for free, but remember, you get what you pay for.

I find that people with "skin in the game" are very motivated to take advantage of all of the systems and processes and worksheets that we've developed over 30 years in the business. And they love getting to do it with others who are doing the same by their side.

Regardless, I do hope you'll find someone who can help walk you through it. At minimum, a coffee or Zoom date with an entrepreneur whose business is sitting where you want yours to go would be helpful.

I would normally recommend asking another speaker, but here's the truth about that. When you are busy running a multi-million-dollar company that involves a lot of travel, it's difficult to squeeze mentoring into your calendar. Any free time you have, you want to spend the majority of it with your family or relaxing. I know there are lots of kind people out there, but please be aware of their time and how precious every free moment is to them.

Finding someone to help you over the trials and tribulations of scaling can be extremely helpful in your journey. Having someone to share the high highs and the low lows is a wonderful thing!

Thought-Provoking Questions

Where will you find your Scaling Mentor?

____

____

____

How invested will your mentor be?

____

____

____

How invested will you be in the process?

____

____

____

My Mentor

A few years ago, I hired Lisa, a business strategy coach to help me sort through some of my next steps. Our work together was very productive. But what I most appreciated Lisa for was her ability to help me see what was possible.

We held our meeting on the balcony of a Florida hotel overlooking the water. Inspired right? And we talked through where I wanted my business to go. In that moment, when she suggested raising my private coaching fees, I couldn't wrap my mind around it. There were also a few other things she recommended I might do that I needed time for my mindset to catch up on.

Fast forward two years, Lisa wrote me an e-mail that said, "I just stumbled across the notes from our meeting on the balcony. Here's a copy of what we mapped out that day." Low and behold, everything that we discussed had already come true. Even the things that in that moment, I could not see happening.

Lisa had a bigger dream for me than I had for myself. She planted the seed, my mindset caught up, I took action and the entire dream became reality. That's the power of having a scaling mentor.

Strategy #3

Create Systems that Operate (and Earn) While You Sleep

There is one puzzle piece that will allow you to scale and grow your business – systems. Without them, it's chaos. Even the simple pieces of your business, like making sure that a contract gets sent out or a check has been received, need a process to follow.

For the purpose of scaling your business, we are going to focus on systems in the following areas:

- CRM
- Customer Service
- Finance
- Marketing
- Sales
- Project Management (Implementation)
- Analytics

CRM (Customer Relationship Management)

Here's a great question for you. How are you managing your clients from the first point of contact and on through, all the way to the speaking engagement and after care?

I hope your answer is a CRM, or Customer Relationship Management!

Many of our students in The Wealthy Speaker School start without a CRM in place. They are using an e-mail and calendar system or spreadsheet to try to manage any prospects that they reach out to. Some even attempt to keep track of things in their memory! (At 56 years old, I can tell you that isn't even remotely an option for me anymore!)

When you fast forward three years, and you've now got thousands of clients instead of hundreds, you're going to want to know a good number of details.

- What is the prospect's title (are they a decision-maker)?
- When is their next live event?
- What month do they plan events?
- Who makes the decision (and how)?
- How many people will attend the event?
- What fee did you quote (and for what specifically)?
- And the list goes on and on.

The goal is to fill in blank fields in your CRM to a degree that you can "merge" the contact into a contract or speaker agreement and have everything you need on the form.

Additionally, you should be able to trace all your interactions with any client to see which of your e-mails were opened and all your notes from every point of contact and conversation.

If none of this is happening now, you'll want to consider getting a CRM so you can grow and scale your speaking business. Check out your Bonus Page for a webinar we did on CRMs if you don't already have one that is working for you.

BONUS PAGE

CRM Webinar: *www.speakerlauncher.com/scale*

We have been using Infusionsoft (now known as Keap) for many years but have recently moved to Active Campaign for our CRM and marketing systems. (See your Bonus Page for more details on this platform.) Active Campaign collects money for us in the form of client payments, monthly subscriptions, book sales, etc. When you're thinking about scaling, you're going to want to consider more options so you can make money while you sleep – that's right, make money while you sleep. (More on this in Strategy #6 on revenue streams.) Some of the paths to get there include online courses, membership communities or mastermind groups.

BONUS PAGE

Active Campaign: *www.speakerlauncher.com/scale*

Moving from a one-to-one model (e.g., coaching) to a one-to-many structure (e.g., online course) is essential for scaling because you only have so much time on the calendar. When you are able to pull in recurring charges or subscriptions, you'll be able to see growth exponentially.

When it comes to scaling, it would be rare for a business to be successful without a strong CRM. My Inner Circle Mastermind member, Frank Somma, is a sales and communication guru who could sell a cape to Superman. He's that good!

SUCCESS STORY

Frank Somma

Customizing Your CRM

Frank believes it is impossible to be successful in selling without utilizing some form of customer relationship management. He has set up his CRM so that it shows him if his e-mails were opened, automates a drip campaign, schedules everything from calls to tasks to speaking dates, tracks details of potential deals, keeps notes, hits him with reminders, and much, much more.

Beyond that, the real beauty of Frank's CRM is the fields he has customized. He calls it Frankie's Fabulous Fourteen. These are fourteen bits of information about his client that allow him to easily personalize his conversation. He stores data about spouses, kids, grandkids, pets, their alma mater, favorite sports teams, hobbies, etc.

And I've seen this firsthand, even when I'm coaching him! When he has a coaching call with me and he asks about Jackson (my dog) by name, we get into conversations about our dogs' training successes and foibles. And when Frank does this with his clients, they feel engaged! And isn't engagement what we're after in every client call?

One caveat here. Frank is genuinely interested in Jackson. He loves the stories about him and listens actively. As Frank's role model Kinky Friedman said, "You can't fake sincerity." This interest in the personal bits about your client can never be an inauthentic ploy intended to move the sale forward. It's got to be genuine or you're only reinforcing the negative stereotype great salespeople spend so much time having to overcome.

Frank uses his CRM in a way that is designed to build engagement – brilliant!!! He currently uses Karma for Speakers as his CRM. (We've put a link on your Bonus Page to a webinar we did with Karma so that you can see the power of a great CRM.)

BONUS PAGE

CRM Webinar: *www.speakerlauncher.com/scale*

Customer Service Systems

Using a CRM is an integral system; customizing it is priceless!

Customer service is an area where some speakers shine and others haven't given it enough thought.

Having a CRM system can be a great start to collecting all the data and storing any touch points with clients. As well, you should have a process in place that either you or a team member follows up to ensure you are staying top of mind with your clients.

An autoresponder (e-mail) that goes out after your engagement is nice. This could be a letter that says thanks and maybe requests a testimonial. Even better, perhaps you set up a "Post Event Debrief" call scheduled in advance. If the client feels like you are going to provide more value, which you should, then they may be more likely to meet with you again. Now your odds of booking more business and getting referrals go up, especially if you have some proposed "recommendations" that they can do to keep the message you delivered live.

This is the power of systems! If every time there is a speaking engagement, consulting contract, new coaching client or someone joining your membership program, each and every step of the customer experience, onboarding engagement and post-gig follow up should be explored and systematized. This takes time and constant tweaking to existing systems. And a good use of analytics, which we'll get to near the end of this chapter.

Thought-Provoking Questions

What is your system for onboarding new clients, keeping them satisfied and following up after an event?

____

____

____

Once you get a client, how are you making sure that they are satisfied enough to tell others about you?

____

____

____

What's your system for collecting future business, referrals and testimonials?

Now, let's think about how your brand plays out in your customer service systems – are your communications clear and is your personality shining through? Exercise 5 can help take your customer service touch points to the next level.

Exercise 5:

CUSTOMER TOUCH POINTS

There are dozens of touch points between you and your customer. Here are some pieces of the system that you might want to review to make sure that they are in place and reflect your brand and personality.

Sales process – initial e-mails all the way through to agreement: Did you remember to sprinkle your personality through those?

Speaking agreement: Is it legal mumbo jumbo? Is your personality in there?

Follow through from contract to play date: Is everything in one place, easy for the client (i.e., everything they need is in one place via your meeting planner's page)?

Post engagement after care – next steps or recommendation call: Do you schedule that in advance?

Onboarding to your course or membership: Is the path clear? Is it going to be fun? Perhaps there's a video?

Customer service – someone has a problem: What's your default? Does everyone on the team know it?

Someone calls your office: Does your voice mail system include personality?

____

____

____

Someone e-mails while you are on vacation: Do autoresponders include your personality?

____

____

____

In each of the customer service touch points we just covered, when it comes to the personality of your brand, let's be intentional about what we are putting out there. What flavor does your brand convey? Exercise 6 will help you explore this important part of your system.

Exercise 6: YOUR BRAND'S PERSONALITY

Here's a checklist that you might use to choose the top three characteristics that could be woven into your systems.

- ☐ fun
- ☐ business-like
- ☐ serious
- ☐ authentic
- ☐ flexible – roll with it
- ☐ empathetic/compassionate
- ☐ strong leader
- ☐ trustworthy – no BS style

- ☐ instill confidence in others
- ☐ confident (you)
- ☐ expert
- ☐ passionate
- ☐ magnetic
- ☐ caring/generous
- ☐ curious
- ☐ approachable

Remember Neen James (from Strategy #2) who was positioned beautifully for growth? Here's an e-mail that I received from her when I asked if I could use her story. BTW, all of Neen's clients know as soon as they've met or heard her that she is Australian and she works that into her personality, even in her out-of-office autoresponder.

> G'day gorgeous,
>
> Today is full of coaching appointments with clients (which is so exciting for me) and they are committed to finish this year strong!
>
> If you need anything for an upcoming virtual event or conference, Sue, our sales goddess, would be delighted to help you: sue@neenjames.com
>
> Have a wonderful day, enjoy this magnificent weather, and remember to create a moment for someone today.
>
> PS: Did you know we now have a coaching program? Find out more here:
>
> https://neenjames.com/product/finish-the-year-strong-coaching-with-neen-james/

Once again Neen has a system in place to ensure that the client's needs are met, and it includes a healthy dose of her personality.

I hope you'll check in with your touch points and customer service systems to see where you might develop or improve.

Finance Systems

Finance is, of course, my favorite system. After all, it's all about money!

As I said, here at Speaker Launcher and The Wealthy Speaker School, we currently use Active Campaign and Woo Commerce as our e-commerce platform and Stripe as our payment processing tool to collect credit card transactions in two currencies (US and Canadian). (Exercise 7 will help you check in on your all-important financial systems.)

Active Campaign's autoresponders allow us to have a system in place for following up on failed credit card transactions – whether this happens when someone is first registering or on a monthly subscription charge. This comes up more than you think as banks are more and more suspicious of fraud. These become recurring income, so you don't want to miss out on these. Some people employ companies to do the follow-up in the voice of the organization. Amy Porterfield, online marketing expert, recommends Gravy Solutions and although I don't use them yet, they seem terrific.

Exercise 7: COLLECTION AND TRACKING

Systems for collecting and tracking money are probably the most important systems of all. Here are a few questions to help you check in with your systems to see where you might need to adjust.

Some of you generate invoices and collect checks – 50% deposit and 50% balance. Do you have a clear system in place for collecting and tracking this?

____

____

____

Do you have it tied into your accounting software, like QuickBooks, so you can easily send invoices and track payments?

____

____

____

Are you running your AR (accounts receivable) report monthly and following up on money not collected in a timely manner?

____

____

____

What's your system for travel reimbursement (i.e., send receipts to VA for billing to clients)? Who is following up to ensure payment is made?

____

____

____

Should you consider credit cards instead of checks? Or, even better, low-fee or no-fee e-mail money transfers?

____

____

____

Anything you repeat should have a system, especially when it comes to collecting money. You might say, "I'd lose 2-3% if I accept credit cards." What if your analytics showed you that getting the money in quicker paid off, and in the end you earned more? That's some research worth doing. Perhaps there's a part of your speaker's agreement that offers several payment options and you request that the client tick the box for the one that will be the fastest/easiest for them?

Figure out a plan that will get the money to you in as quick a fashion as possible, as easily as possible for the client and a system to track it.

The process for all of this should be documented so nothing gets missed. By documenting it clearly and outlining any steps that need to be taken, you or a team member can easily follow up! We'll talk more about SOPs, or Standard Operating Procedures, a little bit later in this chapter.

Many speakers use eSpeakers to help with their systems. As one of the beta testers of the original eSpeakers, originally designed by the amazing Art Berg as a way to keep all of the details about an event in one place, I could see the power of a good checklist. Of course, at the top of that checklist is "Received Deposit" or "Received Balance Due." (Note: eSpeakers has gone far beyond event checklists. Make sure to check out their current offerings. You'll find a link on your Bonus Page.)

BONUS PAGE

eSpeakers: *www.speakerlauncher.com/scale*

This information and every detail about an engagement should be based on the cloud. When you are standing at the baggage claim at the airport, and you can't recall the name of the limo service picking you up (yes, that's right, Wealthy Speakers get limos), opening up an app and seeing all of the details in the palm of your hand is essential. In theory, as long as everything is on the Cloud, the system is secure. If you're notorious for losing your phone or not keeping it charged, why not create a system to travel with a back-up battery!

Marketing Systems

Marketing is likely the system that gets the most attention (see Exercise 8). But is your marketing consistent? We do e-mail broadcasts weekly on Tuesdays and release podcast recordings every Thursday. This has been happening like clockwork for years and the consistency pays off.

> *The marketing that counts the most is marketing done on a regular schedule.*

This is what fills your funnel and keeps new clients coming your way.

Exercise 8:
A SYSTEM FOR MARKETING

Your marketing system should take the aspects discussed below into consideration.

E-mail Marketing

How often are you reaching out to your list? And when specifically (i.e., every Tuesday 1 PM ET)?

____

____

____

How often do you tell your list about new products or services or "ask for the business?"

____

____

____

Social Media

What is your plan for the consistent posting of relevant information on the platforms that have the greatest impact on your business? Which platforms will you focus on?

____

____

____

Do you stick to a content calendar or make it up as you go?

____

____

____

List Building/Lead Generation

How are you drawing new people into your community and onto your e-mail list?

____

____

____

How do you move people out of social media (Instagram, Facebook, LinkedIn, YouTube) over to your website? Is there a consistent strategy?

____

____

____

Sure, new followers on Instagram are nice, but you are competing with millions of other Insta-influencers. Being able to speak to your customer directly via e-mail is still a great idea! Are you developing new lead magnets to get people on your list?

____

____

____

Every speaking engagement (virtual or live) is an opportunity to add tens, hundreds and sometimes thousands of new fans to your base. Are you taking advantage?

____

____

____

Adding e-mails from the majority of the people in every audience is a system that is high priority. If you're not doing this, you're missing out on thousands of warm prospects to whom you could be marketing new speeches or selling anything new that you launch. Some of my School members are using TalkBook to collect e-mail addresses from their audiences. There are many apps out there to assist with this task.

Are you capitalizing by using "text to" software or the more basic collection of business cards or a form?

____

____

____

Product Launches

I find launches to be difficult, mainly because we have so many products and offerings. My beautiful *Wealthy Speaker Daily Success Planner & Journal* is the Cinderella of my offerings, rarely getting any attention, yet it's a wonderful product. We just don't have enough room on the marketing calendar for one more launch. When you are constantly "pitching" to your list, you risk losing them.

How are you introducing new products and services to your list to get the biggest bang for your buck?

____

____

____

The system I'd recommend is a marketing calendar. Having a master plan is essential – a plan where you know each month all that is being promoted (or launched), what you are writing about (if you have a blog), what topic you are podcasting on (if you have a podcast) and if you have a theme for the month that may also play out in your social media. This system will allow your followers to see there is some method to your madness.

I mentioned Amy Porterfield a few pages earlier. After being in her world for several years, you'll see the same things circling back around at the same time each year. She'll promote one of her programs, like Digital Course Academy, and does a great job with a pretty aggressive combination of lead magnets (like a Masters Class), e-mail campaigns and webinars to launch. Then, several months later, once her program is up and running, she might promote one of her affiliates, like Marie Forleo's B School.

When it comes to marketing, having a solid strategy and processes in place, as opposed to the spray and pray method, will do wonders for your bottom line. Consider putting a marketing calendar in place to help keep all of your marketing initiatives straight and to measure what works and what doesn't.

Sales Systems

Sales systems will likely have the most impact on your finances. Keeping your outbound efforts consistent is often the more difficult part of the sales process.

Keeping Your Funnel Full

Many of you have heard me talk about how Kindra launched her business with 600 e-mails to associations. We'll include a link to my podcast with Kindra sharing her start-up story and her journey to success on your Bonus Page.

She targeted the American Marketing Association to begin with, which was a good fit for her storytelling message.

That effort spun into many other audiences and speaking opportunities. Then, when Kindra wanted to add *more* leads to her funnel, she went back and did another 600.

Today, she has systems in place to do that on a regular basis. Social media, e-mail marketing campaigns, lead magnets and sales outreach are all a part of her ongoing strategy.

BONUS PAGE

Kindra Hall Podcast: *www.speakerlauncher.com/scale*

How Do You Keep Your Sales Funnel Full?

Here at The Wealthy Speaker School, we have a very simple system for engaging new students. Several times a year, we run a live webinar for emerging speakers. We target people new to the business because we want to welcome people into the School early and keep them growing with us throughout their careers. We give them some solid information during our one-hour webinar, and then do a pitch for the School at the end. Sometimes the pitch has just one simple call to action, a chat with one of our team members.

When you find something that works, you double down. That's what it takes to scale.

Once we have our webinar recorded, we set up an "evergreen" system to run it on demand and purchase Facebook and Instagram ads to pull people into the webinar. As soon as we find an ad that works or a webinar that works particularly well, we double the ad spend.

SUCCESS STORY

David Avrin

Creating the System

My friend David shared with me his system for booking speaking engagements. He and his business manager, Tiffany, identify a list of prospects that they want to market to for bookings. They share a raw list with their research team (outsourcing overseas often makes this quite affordable) and ask them to fill in a spreadsheet with all of the particulars – questions like: When was their last meeting? When is their next meeting? Who is the person in charge of speakers? Who did they hire for last year's conference? When will they be making speaker selection? Etcetera.

David's system even includes which days of the week are reserved for outreach, which are for research and which days are spent on follow-up with prospects. This consistent outbound approach puts David on main stages 60+ times per year consistently (barring global or country-wide crises).

And by keeping the wheels of this operation moving throughout the year, he is going to get results.

Thought-Provoking Questions

What is your commitment to consistency in your marketing system?

____

____

____

How will you connect directly with clients on a regular basis?

____

____

____

Project Management and Implementation Systems

How do you make sure that your projects move from start to finish? What are your systems for implementing new initiatives and following through? Check out Exercise 9.

Those of you who are project managers know that there are a lot of moving parts to get a project from start through to completion. Our team uses Asana as a project management tool, but there are many good tools out there. I'm visual, so I like something pretty. ☺

Whenever I have a new project or task, I place it in Asana and assign someone on the team to complete the project. They can ask me questions inside the tool, share links, files and updates and, finally, mark it complete. If I'm ever wondering, "Hey, what happened to that brilliant idea I had for marketing?" I can just look at my list of projects inside Asana and see what's been completed. There are opportunities to collaborate inside Asana and I love that several people can work on a project together.

Recently, I brought in someone new to manage our Facebook ads. (More on hiring the right team in Strategy #5.) As we onboarded our new teammate, I could see her dialogue with our team leader through Asana. Based on the questions she was asking and the recommendations she made, I was confident that we had hired a good fit. Being able to watch the project conversation unfold was essential to shoring up my confidence and thus putting more money towards the Facebook Ads project. The goal isn't to micromanage projects, but to lead them. And having benchmarks and timelines in place allows us to know when projects go off the rails.

The success of your projects is only as good as your system for implementation.

Exercise 9:

HOW ARE YOU MANAGING YOUR PROJECTS?

If you're having conversations over e-mail, I'd recommend that you find a tool that works to place everything about a project into one place. And make sure that you share your vision (your "why") for a project first.

Here are a few questions that you can take into any project.

What do you want to accomplish with this project? Why are you doing it?

____

____

____

What does the completed project (success) look like? How will you know it worked?

____

____

____

What would be the worst case scenario?

____

____

____

If you find yourself not making any headway on projects, you need to look at:

Team

Are they doing what you need them to do?

____

____

____

Systems

Is the system for following a project from start to end working?

____

____

____

Leadership

Are you leading the project well or getting in the way by micromanaging?

____

____

____

Reducing Your E-mail

If you're anything like me, you can wake up to 50 e-mails in your in-box and it makes you want to go straight back to bed. E-mail can be so overwhelming. So, what do we do? We have a system!

Some of you may have your assistant screen and weed out any e-mails that don't require your attention. I'm not there yet, but I can see it on the horizon. I probably get only ten e-mails a day that require my attention. The rest are ads from service providers that I use, tests of broadcasts that are going out, people who want something from me, etc. All e-mails from the website go straight to my assistant so that cuts back significantly. But nearly everything we do gets a response from a template that is set up already.

For instance, if someone wants to be a guest on our podcast, first they fill out our Guest Inquiry Form, and then it goes into one of three buckets and my assistant sends out the appropriate e-mail based on which response we're going to give them.

Someone e-mails me directly to schedule a chat with me. At some point we won't do this anymore, but we have an e-mail that lays out two options. A 15-minute "Next Steps" call or a "Focus 40" – a 40-minute coaching session. (Notice how we name everything in our business? You should be doing the same.)

One thing that reduces my e-mail tremendously is Slack, a team communication tool we use for one-off questions and to communicate good news. For instance, my assistant Monica wants to know if I need to move a School coaching call because it lands on my vacation week. Those are easy questions that would take so much longer during an e-mail exchange. Using Slack, which is like Instant Messaging or Texting, has made a significant impact on my in-box.

Because Slack has Channels, we can place a message inside the most appropriate area. We have channels set up for each team member, but also for social media, Facebook ads, our School, payment issues, analytics, team, etc. For instance, if I see there's a message inside payment issues, I already know that it's going to be about a credit card that's declined and where it is in the process of getting collected. And if I'm ever curious, I can just look in that channel and see what's outstanding.

Standard Operating Procedures (SOP)

We have systems for everything! And you might think that feels cumbersome, but with hundreds (or thousands) of people in our School, and questions coming in daily from students, we have to have a Standard Operating Procedure (SOP) in place for everything.

If we added a new team member to the School to handle student inquiries, they should be able to read our SOP manual and know exactly how to handle each issue that could arise. These are the types of things that we don't want to be figuring out when our School is chockablock; we want to have this all well in hand when we double and triple our number of students.

Perhaps you don't have an online course or membership. What does this look like for you in your current business model? If someone left, would you be in crisis because they took all of the passwords and procedures for something with them?

SUCCESS STORY
Rhonda Scharf

Managing Your Protocols

My good friend Rhonda has a healthy speaking, training and webinar business. She focuses on administration professionals and is known as the go-to expert in that field. She's got many moving parts and team members in her business.

Last year, tragedy struck when a key team member, David, a young man in his 30s had a heart attack. Rhonda and her husband Warren (who works in the business) were floored by the unexpected loss of their friend who they had worked with for nearly a decade. Then, suddenly they realized that David had been the sole custodian of all the processes and passwords for Rhonda's webinars. They did not have a central location or SOP and it took them several weeks to bring all of the pieces of the puzzle together.

Losing a team member is an incredibly emotional experience, but what came out of it for Rhonda's business was something positive. Today, Rhonda's company has a protocol in place for all passwords and operating procedures. Any team member could step in and take over anyone else's role with ease.

Thought-Provoking Questions

Who is holding the secrets for your business?

____

____

____

And if it's you, do you have an emergency document in place for those left behind should you be out of commission?

____

____

____

In Case of Emergency

What would happen if you were incapacitated? For many years, I've kept an "in case of emergency" folder in our safe at home. It contains my master password (which is the key to everything in my business and all of the passwords), who to get in touch with about all of the areas of the business and instructions should the business need to be shut down. This is aside from our SOPs. What would your family do if something unexpected happened? Are you prepared?

Analytics Systems to Measure Your Efforts

Analyzing your efforts is probably the least sexy of all of the systems, but possibility one of the most important. If you don't analyze the data, then how do you know how you're doing and what works and what doesn't?

As an example, we use Simplecast to host and to collect our podcast statistics. It allows us to see what podcast channels and devices are most popular (spoiler alert, it's Apple Podcasts and iPhones) and which podcast topics get the most downloads. We also analyze our website traffic and other metrics using Google Analytics. This data helps us to know who is coming to our site, what drove them there (us, someone else or a search), where they are coming from and where we are losing people. Understanding these metrics allows us to know more about what our customers want – and what we need to fix.

This year we decided to build and run a mini-course that would be a lead magnet. It would give people a little glimpse into The Wealthy Speaker School. But guess what our analytics showed us? People weren't getting through the three videos. They would stall out. We concluded that unless you have "skin in the game" (i.e., an investment) you might not follow through an entire course.

Think about it. How often have you crapped out of something that took time and energy when you hadn't paid for it? I know I signed up for a free university class that I never attended (for whatever reason) and didn't feel bad about it. Why? Because I had nothing invested. I wonder maybe if the university had charged, even a small amount, if I would have completed the course? Hard to say.

You can use analytics to measure:

- website traffic,
- key words (search engine optimization),
- podcast listenership,
- blog readership,
- e-mail open rates,
- e-mail sign ups (magnet success),
- video views, and
- advertising results.

I have a confession to make; analytics is one of my least favorite things. I know I need to pay better attention personally to this piece of our system. To make up for my lack of interest, I have my team bring me analytics to each meeting. They can't be ignored! This is my version of "forced analysis" and it works for us, but I know I can always be doing better.

And let me be clear, we can be doing better at everything. We do not have a business without flaws. And setting up all of these systems definitely wasn't all me. I attribute the majority of our systems and processes to my team leader, Carolyn Crummey of Virtasktic, and my assistant, Monica Martin, for being the implementer.

We're showing you what we're doing so that you might consider what's right for you. We're not saying that we have it all together. To think that any business has all their sh*t together is laughable. We all have flaws, weaknesses, areas for improvement.

Strategy #4

Subtract In Order to Add

It Isn't Always About Adding

I first heard the phrase "subtract in order to add" from Dan Sullivan. He was talking about teams when he wrote a blog called "Multiplication by Subtraction." The idea is that you might be able to grow your business faster if you let go of team members who aren't serving you.

My friend Rob who owns a company that makes plush toys for the promotional products world kept his bookkeeper on for 17 years. For 15 of those 17 years he wanted to let her go. He didn't like her as a person and she did sloppy bookkeeping. But Rob kept putting it off and putting it off. Finally, he pulled the trigger and it was far easier than he even imagined. Once this happened and he put the right team in place, his company was able to soar!

We're going to take "subtract in order to add" beyond your team, but we'll place a link to Dan's article on your Bonus Page.

BONUS PAGE

Dan Sullivan, "Multiplication by Subtraction":
www.speakerlauncher.com/scale

We don't need to say a lot about this strategy, because it's a simple one. For me, it spurs the concept that sometimes in order to grow, subtracting from the equation is required. Perhaps there's a client that you've held onto for far longer than was warranted or a revenue stream that you've outgrown or, like Rob, there is a team member who really needed to go.

Letting go may be helpful in order to grow.

Busy, Busy, Busy

In the speaking profession, I see a lot of people doing "busy" work – work that allows them to say, "Oh, I'm so busy." If probed, it turns out that this work isn't very profitable.

How often have you been to a speaker's conference (during normal times) and every second speaker you talk to is "sooooo busy?" I'd love to hear people saying the opposite. "Yeah, I'm not working that hard, but I'm profitable as heck." That's what being an entrepreneur is all about! If you're not creating the lifestyle of your dreams, if your business is running you rather than the other way around, then this is the time for change!

It's easy for someone whose income is from speaking to look busy. They are flying all over the place delivering presentations. But the numbers on the profit and loss statement are the only thing that count.

Have you ever read *The 4-Hour Workweek* by Timothy Ferriss? It's been years since I picked up my copy of that book, but I do remember the impact it had on me. I have never been one to wear busy as a badge of honor. I knew early on that I didn't want to kill myself earning an above-average income, but reading that book brought all of my instincts to the forefront. He says, "Focus on being productive instead of busy." We've all heard the term "work smarter not harder" – this puts it on steroids.

Think about how much you are able to accomplish on the day before you go on vacation. Why is this time so productive while other days are not? Because you have pared down your list to only the priorities. You've subtracted in order to add.

Tim Ferris also says, "Never automate something that can be eliminated, and never delegate something that can be automated or streamlined." Examine your operation in detail and see where you might tighten things up and perhaps let a few things go.

When it comes to subtracting in order to add, it can help to constantly ask the question "Why are we doing this?"

Right now our goal is to look at what in your business needs to be eliminated and what needs to stay. Of course, we'll talk a lot about letting go of clients – they are the low hanging fruit and might be some of the first to go. But we might also talk about revenue streams that don't make your heart sing. Remember that clutter that was underneath your bed? You forgot that it was there but it was taking up mental space – let's clean out that clutter!

Letting Go So that You Can Grow

Do you have areas of your business that not only don't give you joy, but suck the life right out of you? When you wake in the morning as an entrepreneur, you want to be excited for each and every thing that crosses your desk during the day. Of course, there might be bookkeeping or analysis that isn't your favorite thing, but the big chunks of work that you are doing should have you bouncing off the sheets in the morning.

What about the tough times?

Of course, when something unexpected happens in your business, an illness, a divorce, a pandemic or an economic downturn, you may add a few things back into the mix out of necessity for the short term. But the goal for scaling is that you are doing the work that you love and therefore passion and profits go hand in hand.

There really are two choices when it comes to all of the income you bring in. Subtract it (i.e., let it go) or love it and appreciate it. You'll read more about this in Strategy #10. I'm okay with either choice you make – but my goal is for you to be intentional about it.

SUCCESS STORY

Dr. Angela Mulrooney

Letting Go in Order to Grow

Angela arrived at my doorstep as a private coaching client feeling overwhelmed. She had three distinct buckets in her business. Two she loved, but one, her dental consulting practice, left her feeling dissatisfied. She loved talking to the dentists, the leaders of the organization, but when it came to going into a practice to implement the changes she helped to map out, she knew she wasn't the best person for that job.

The willingness to let go of something can be pivotal in your growth. It's when you can't see it any other way that you get stuck.

So, the first step was being willing to let go of that chunk of business. Could she live without it? The answer was a resounding "yes" and it offered Angela massive relief to let it go.

That action freed her from the sense of being overwhelmed long enough to realize that she didn't have to throw the baby out with the bathwater. She kept the leader consulting piece for herself and brought in a partner to help implement the rest of the on-site work with the practices. Someone who she thought was far better at the work than she was! Win-win!

Subtract in Order to Grow

Finally, let's take a look at anything in your business that needs to go away, so that you can grow. Let me give you some examples.

You've been using a CRM (Customer Relationship Management) that isn't serving you and you have a love-hate relationship with. When you put the right piece of technology in place that's a good fit for you, and really learn it and use it, it will serve you incredibly well in the long term.

Perhaps there's an outdated system that you have been running – like managing your own calendar instead of taking it to technology with Calendly or one of the online calendar systems. When you grow, you are going to need those minutes or hours that you spend each month going back and forth with clients to schedule time, especially if you are scheduling a lot of discovery calls or coaching clients.

Maybe you've been collecting names and e-mail addresses manually at your live events for years but it's time to move to a "text to" system so that you eliminate the need to place those names into your database and it happens automatically.

Some of you have created social media channels or paths that seemed like a good idea at the time, but you've never put any energy into them. Perhaps you need to take down some old videos on YouTube? Or close out a social media account that isn't serving you? Or the newsletter that you've never followed up on? All of this is like that clutter under your bed. It's eating away precious mental energy and letting go will be a huge relief. You know what I'm talking about, don't you?

There's likely something that you are doing in your business, that you've been doing for years, that you know needs to either go away or be replaced with something that will be more in line with your growth. It's either a "Heck yeah!" or a "Hell no!" – you decide! Use Exercise 10 to explore this idea.

Exercise 10: GROWING BY SUBTRACTING

Here are a few questions that will help you wrap up this piece.

What revenue streams are not serving you?

____

____

____

Which clients can you say goodbye to in order to make room for right fit clients?

____

____

____

What old processes, systems or technology do you need to subtract from your business in order to multiply?

____

____

____

Strategy #5

Creating that Kick Butt Team

Is it possible to have a seven-figure business without anyone helping you? I think so. I've talked to Joe Calloway about this on numerous occasions, and he has always opted to work alone. However, I think that Joe is more the exception than the rule.

Solopreneur

Over 30 years in the speaking business, and he did it all himself. His story is below, but there's a footnote to Joe's story. He began the process of closing his business down in March of 2019 and concluded the final pieces of business in July of 2020. He's going to be focusing more on some starts-ups he's involved with and on managing his real estate investments.

A Team of One

For Joe, one of the great joys of the speaking business was that it's the simplest business in the world. At least it was the way he did it.

No employees. No virtual assistants. No marketing team or speaker management company. Just him.

So, how did Joe do it?

He spoke directly to every bureau agent, client and prospect about potential or booked speeches. He didn't want anyone getting between himself and the client. Having that direct communication made not only for excellent relationships, but for effective decisions.

Also, he booked his own travel. Joe confessed to being very particular about times, connections, etc., and with everything available on the internet it took only a few minutes at most to book even the most complicated trip. And it was exactly the way he wanted it.

Beyond that, what took most of his time – was writing the speeches. Each one was unique in that Joe did extensive client research and customized every presentation. That took about 50% of his time.

What about selling? Joe's marketing and selling approach was all repeat and referral focused. He sold by doing a great job on stage, and letting positive client word of mouth drive business to him.

Scaling and Your Time

I always like to show that for every idea, there's an opposite idea that can also work. We can see from Joe's 30-year journey that solo is possible. He kept his offerings very lean and mean – speeches and books. And because his fee was high ($30K), it worked.

This business is yours to build based on what's perfect for you. You may read Joe's story and think, "That's it. I don't need to go any further!" And that's okay.

However, based on what I've been learning over the past decade, a team is indeed required to build the scaled version of the company of your dreams. In my own experience, when it comes to running all of the moving pieces of my business I want to have the best people in place for each area. More likely than not, I am not the person who is best to do the majority of these jobs.

Think about it. If you charge $500-$1500/hour, as many experts, including me, do, you have a clear handle on the value of your time.

Yet many of us are still doing the $30/hour jobs.

So, what should you be spending your time doing? Well, I typically break it down into four areas and everything outside of these four things gets delegated to the team.

Creating

You might call this writing, or you might call it content creation. Creating could even be the time you spend sitting and thinking (that's pretty important). It can be designing and developing new content for delivery, writing blog posts or articles, prepping for podcasts, creating deliverables for consulting work, copywriting for marketing, the list goes on. As experts, we are constantly pumping out new material.

Another part of creating is the roadmap for the future of your company. Making decisions on where you want to go in the future, setting goals and timelines is huge. The one thing I see many "busy" speakers neglect is business planning and strategy. Pausing the work "in" your business to work "on" the business. I heard a cool quote recently from SP Solutions. "When you work 'in' your business, you're working on today's income. When you work 'on' your business, you're working on tomorrow's income."

Selling

Sure, it's a nice idea to have someone else do the selling for you, but the majority of my clients are the rainmakers for their companies. As is often the case, no one is able to sell you, like you. It's nice to think about handing off the sales role, but some of you will feel that loss of interaction with clients more than others. As you grow, it may be that only "high stakes" sales come across your desk and everything else is passed along to someone else.

Back in my bureau days, when I ran the exclusives division of the speakers bureau in Dallas, Joe Calloway and I were good friends, and we invited him to come on board exclusively with our bureau. After about six months, however, Joe and I agreed it wasn't a good fit. He really missed the interaction with the clients and other bureau agents. Joe didn't recognize until that moment how much the relationship part of the business – the selling – meant to him.

Sales is a big part of my role in my company, and I enjoy this piece. When I approach a call with a prospect with curiosity (thank you Chris West for this intention), I can see which of our tools or services is the right fit for them. That's fun for me. And making a sale is fun. I farm out some of the pieces, like the selling of The Wealthy Speaker School goes to Jen who leads our School. She's the first face they are going to see when they arrive in the School, so I think that makes sense.

A part of our sales process is to deliver what we call "Focus 40" sessions. This meeting gives our clients an opportunity to have a coaching session at a reduced rate, and then five minutes at the end might be set aside for recommendations and next steps. This is when I get to sell! If you have coaching as a part of your offering, you may want to consider adding a specially priced session. (I don't love offering free coaching sessions as it brings a lot of tire kickers to your door and people should be prepared to pay handsomely for working with you.) Please note, coaching sessions are different than client discovery calls.

Delivering

This is likely where many of you have the most fun – delivering your offerings. Giving a speech or a workshop, coaching or consulting with a client directly, anything that transpires between you and a client would be considered delivery.

Virtual presentations and webinars would also go under delivery. I know many people thrive on live events, but I believe virtual will be a part of meetings for the foreseeable future.

Leading

It's not always conscious when you move from solopreneur to leader of your company. Perhaps it starts with one hire, an admin person or VA (virtual assistant), and then expands from there. My goal is to make "being the leader of your organization" top of mind so that each and every hire is impactful and that you lead them towards your vision of the future from the day they begin.

Thought-Provoking Question

Think about what kind of culture you want to create inside your organization. Some considerations might include: a culture of learning and growing (especially from mistakes), positivity, fun, efficiency, team oriented, etc.

Now write down the type of culture that you want to create.

____

____

____

____

____

____

Of course, a piece of leading is delegating and deciding who does what. That may become very important as you grow. The more you can keep job roles clear and communicate with everybody who does what, the easier life will be.

As an entrepreneur who wants to scale, those are the four areas where you want to concentrate your time. Things that don't fall into these categories may get delegated to team members. You'll see during our Time Audit exercise below that simply bringing an awareness to how you are spending your time is extremely powerful.

As you lead your company, team will become more and more important, but so is ensuring that your finances are safe.

Checks and Balances

One important part of leading may be signing paychecks for everyone. Please note that I said *signing*, not writing or figuring out payroll deductions (if you have employees and not self-employed contractors).

Being a great leader doesn't mean delegating so much that you put your head in the sand about your numbers.

I recall Oprah saying, "Delegate everything but signing of the checks and opening the bank statement." Doing these tasks allows you to keep an eye on the money. Another part of leading will be to check in on the P&L (profit and loss statement) on a regular basis and make sure that you are on track with your numbers.

And as Vince Poscente found out the hard way, you want to balance delegation with checks and balances.

SUCCESS STORY

Vince Poscente

Keeping Your Eye on the Numbers

Back when Vince had a real job, as he likes to put it, he realized how much he disliked being micromanaged. It defined how he would lead in his own business. Although trust is at the core of working with others, Vince learned the hard way, to the tune of over

> $50,000, that a financial system of checks and balances sets up the foundation for trust.
>
> About ten years into business Vince hired an assistant who was able to multitask while having a superb interface with his clients. What he didn't realize was that she was creatively paying off her credit cards with corporate funds. It was a financial game of Jenga as each personal payment she pulled out would come crashing down at tax time.
>
> When Vince's CPA came in to reconcile the finances, his crooked assistant left "for personal reasons." They quickly changed their system of checks and balances while Vince hired a new assistant. The new assistant was fully aware of how he took her predecessor to court. Trust had a new verb attached. "Trust and Verify." Vince still doesn't micromanage, but he does ensure his systems of money-flow facilitate maximum trust.

Of course, Vince's story is a cautionary tale and you might think that this is a good case *against* delegating more of your tasks. But please don't let this stop you. This situation is an outlier, and I hope that you will put checks and balances into place so that this could never happen in your business.

Now there are a few things that might have gotten missed, but hopefully the bulk of your time can be wrapped into those four categories outlined earlier in this Chapter: writing, selling, delivering and leading.

But, to really understand how you are spending the bulk of your time, consider doing a time audit (see Exercise 11).

Audit Your Time

The goal here is business growth, and in order to grow you need to manage your time. Use Exercise 11 to discover how you spend your time over the course of a week.

Exercise 11: AUDIT YOUR TIME

Set up a cheat sheet to monitor your time over the course of a day and a week.

Put a piece of paper right beside your laptop and write on it every time you finish a task to document how long you spent and on what. Or at the end of each day add to a note in your phone that summarizes how you spent your time. (That one wouldn't work for me because I can barely remember why I walked into a room, let alone how I spent my time for an entire day.)

Here is a sample chart all ready for you to use.

Time	Task

After you have several days down on paper, a pattern will emerge and you can circle back and review.

Here's a sample day that we can examine.

Time	Task
8:00-9:00	morning routine (journal, exercise, reading)
9:00-10:00	book travel, send client contracts, draft invoices
10:00-11:00	client call

11:00-1:00	break – walk the dog and lunch
1:00-2:00	finish blog post, start another
2:00-3:00	client follow ups, e-mails and calls, write proposals
3:00-4:00	ship product to engagement, fulfill orders, mail books

If you go back to review this example day, what do you notice? What glares out at me is that two entire hours on this day were spent doing $20-$30/hour jobs. Booking travel, client contracts, invoicing, shipping product to engagements or to customers is something that could be delegated. So let's say your time is worth $850/hour, you've just invested $1700 into what should have been $60. Does that make any sense to you?

"But, but, but, Jane! I like my travel booked just a certain way." So you train someone on what all of your little travel peccadilloes are, so they know that you don't like the middle seat or to fly in too late in the day. This isn't rocket science here. It's communication. And if you can't trust someone with your travel, it's very likely you are going to micromanage everything in your business which will make it very hard to scale.

Technology Rather than Team

There are also technology solutions that we can bring into play here – rather than initially hiring.

For instance, you can use a scheduling app to allow clients to choose their time in your calendar. This process alone probably saves me four to six hours a month going back and forth with clients on coaching dates and times. We use Acuity, but it's a very robust calendar system designed for multiple calendars and different types of appointments. There are other simpler systems like Time Trade or Calendly that can work just as well for less complex situations.

For those of you who really like to control your time, when using an online calendar you simply mark out the times that you don't want to be available for client calls. Once you try these things, you'll wonder how you lived without them.

Perhaps there is software you can purchase to help figure out consulting contracts or apps you can download to keep all of your travel expenses in one place. I know that you can scan your receipts right into QuickBooks,® which is a huge time saver.

One app that a busy traveler can't live without, in my opinion, is TripIt.® When your travel gets booked (hopefully by your assistant or VA), he or she e-mails the itinerary to plans@tripit.com and a trip is created. Having your flight, ground transportation and hotel information all in one place is beautiful (some of you use eSpeakers, which integrates with TripIt® nicely). I pay for an upgraded version because when my flight gets canceled the app shows me all of my alternate flight options for rebooking.

There are likely a lot of apps that can make your life easier. The goal is to have systems and processes in place for just about everything that you do on a regular basis so that your time is spent doing the most important things.

Hiring the Right Fit Team

I think that's always our goal – to hire for the "right fit" for each job. In my business, we've done a pretty good job of determining the core competencies of each person on our team (we have five team members) and make sure that they get to work within their strengths for the majority of their time.

Have you ever noticed that a task that someone doesn't want to do gets pushed back on the priority pile again and again? My husband is a great example. In his electrical contracting company, he likes doing all of the actual electrical work, but when it comes to billing and paying the government, he's not all that excited. Therefore, it gets delayed and delayed leaving him constantly in a position of "catch up."

Strategy #6

Choose Revenue Streams that You Love

As business owners, we start out trying to please everyone. It's natural; you flow where the river of business takes you. Sometimes you end up in the weeds, in areas that you don't really enjoy.

"But, Jane, they call it work for a reason." Yeah, whatever!

You decided to be an entrepreneur to build the life and business that was perfect for you. The business of your dreams. Your goal, when choosing revenue streams – offerings of products or services – is to come to a crossroad where passion meets profit. If you are making a ton of money doing work that you hate, how is that going to work long term? More on this in a minute.

If your business is running you, versus you running your business, you have some work to do!

Back in 2011, I heard Dan Sullivan give an interview on Voices of Experience (via The National Speakers Association). He said some things that really caused a paradigm shift in me. It changed the way I coached and ran my business. He said (apologies for the paraphrasing) that if your income consists (only) of you trading your time for money – getting paid to speak – then you basically just have yourself a well-paid job, not a business.

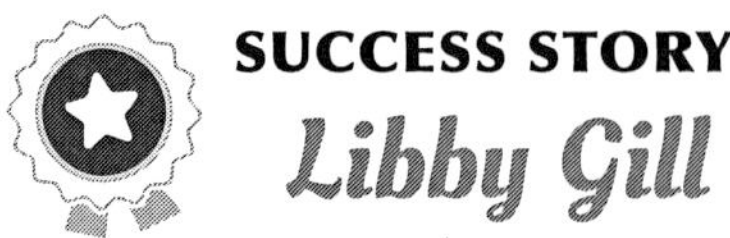

SUCCESS STORY
Libby Gill

Finding the Perfect Staff

My former client, Libby, was an executive coach and speaker who headed communications for Sony, Universal and Turner Broadcasting in her prior career. She told me that building an effective team was critical to her success in both her corporate and entrepreneurial lives. As an executive, she was able to rise quickly through the ranks because of her ability to build world-class teams.

She looked for candidates with a mix of "hard skills," that is, the specific competencies and expertise required for each role. But she also looked for emotional intelligence, those rock star soft skills like collaboration, flexibility and sense of purpose. In addition to checking references carefully – what you see is not always what you get – Libby would ask herself if she could happily fly across country sitting next to this person and still want to go to dinner with them afterward.

In the entrepreneurial world, where Libby recently hit her 20-year anniversary, she says that building an effective team may be even more important than in the corporate world. Your reputation and economic livelihood depend not just on you but also on the people with whom you surround yourself. A sales or marketing person who turns off a buyer or an operations manager who can't create systems can waste a lot of money for a business and a lot of time for a business owner. Libby advises that speakers, "Identify the roles and responsibilities for every potential hire, create a crystal-clear job description and define metrics for success in advance." That way, everyone wins.

I love that Libby suggests metrics for success. If you don't know what success looks like, then how will you know that you've achieved it?

It's not uncommon for people to hire to solve problems. Let's take a look at that next.

Hire for Problems Already Solved

I need to attribute this idea to Brooke Castillo, and please note that Brooke would be the first to say that many of her ideas originated with her mentors. Ironically, one of those mentors is Dan Sullivan. Full circle there!

Brooke talks about not trying to hire to solve problems. That might feel counterintuitive but it actually makes sense.

I often hear, "I'm not getting enough bookings. I want someone to sell speeches for me." Okay, so the problem is that you are not getting booked enough. Over my 30 years in the business, I've seen hundreds of speakers try to hire the position of "booking agent" only to be disappointed.

Why? Because it's the blind leading the blind. The onus is on the booking agent to figure out the process that works.

On the other hand, if you have a system that works for finding and booking business, like my friend David Avrin does (refer to Strategy #3), then you can plug someone into any part of the system and see results. Now the pressure is on the system to work, rather than for that one person to come in and solve your problem.

See the difference?

Another example is finding that perfect assistant or VA (virtual assistant).

This is likely the lowest cost position with the highest payoff. Say it takes you two hours each week to sort through your receipts and get things into your accounting system. You just hand that job over and wash your hands of that work.

But it could even go as far as having someone pick up your dry cleaning. Why? Because you'll be busy running a seven-figure company and that is not a good use of your time. People with multi-million-dollar companies

know that they don't want to spend time doing $20/hour jobs like grocery shopping and sometimes even hire out the cooking to a chef.

A good assistant can take care of all of these things for you. But guess what. Having systems in place first is likely your best starting position.

I refer you to another podcast on your Bonus Page, featuring Brooke and her assistant.

Your ability to hire well is based on the strength of the job description you create and how clear you are about your needs.

BONUS PAGE

Brooke Castillo and Her Assistant:
www.speakerlauncher.com/scale

Test Your Hires

How often do we hire someone and then give them a giant pile of tasks all at once thinking that this is the solution? And what happens? They fail. I like to start out a relationship with a date first, rather than jumping right in to bed. For instance, we might begin with an assignment. I see how well the person does with the project, and then build from there.

A while back, I was looking for someone to help with Facebook ads. My first hire, we'll call him Terry, was someone who didn't take instructions especially well. Luckily, my team caught a lot of Terry's mistakes. It was a good lesson for me because my role in the failure was that I wasn't entirely clear on the mission. Hire failed.

Being willing to fail at hiring is essential to scaling.

The next time around, we gave the new person, Andrea, one task. We were putting on a webinar to launch The Wealthy Speaker School. We had Andrea run Facebook ads to promote the webinar as phase one of the project. Because of the first failed hire, we were very clear on what the goal was and how we would measure success. Our ads led someone to the webinar, then the webinar led to a call with our team member, which led to them joining our School.

We spent $500 on ads (aside from the management fee paid to Andrea). The ads paid for themselves with two new students. I watched the Asana (project management tool) thread between my team and Andrea more closely this time. I could see she was asking the right questions and my confidence grew. When I saw on a Sunday that Andrea had gone into the ads to tweak and adjust (which is a constant in Facebook), I knew we had a winner.

That particular $500 ad spend resulted in 100 new additions to our database, 200 people signed up for the webinar. Fifty people showed up live and the rest went into an autoresponder campaign that resulted in more booked calls with our team leader. And, the end result was that we added eight new people to the School (some paid annually at $1000), which meant the process was successful.

If you're looking for a Facebook ads specialist, we'll put Andrea's information on your Bonus Page under Facebook Advertising as we are happy to refer her.

BONUS PAGE

Facebook Advertising: *www.speakerlauncher.com/scale*

Bottom line: I had much more clarity about my hire based on a failure. I started very slowly and now have someone in place who can truly help us move the needle. If you want to hire team members who can help you scale, start with a project or test that allows you to see how well they do. If they pass, then you start building from there.

Where to Hire

Once you have clarity around what the position requires, one of the best places to find recruits is in your audiences. Always keep your eyes open for talented people who approach you from your audience with, "I really love what you are doing." Often, they want to help and even if you don't have a job in that moment, you might find a new hire that you can nurture and grow as you build your business.

What are the positions we might hire for?

With each new hire, your goal is to uncover their strengths and see if you have a fit.

- Assistant (virtual or local)
- Personal assistant
- Customer liaison/gig coordinator
- Content management (someone who pushes your blog/writing content out)
- Podcast management
- Social media
- Product manager
- Consulting project coordinator
- Research assistant
- Office manager
- Course management
- Community or membership coordinator
- Project manager or implementer
- Business manager
- Sales person
- Graphic design
- Website manager
- Database/broadcast administrator

Those are just a few that you may consider. Many people, like your web and graphic designers, may work for you on a project basis only. It is nice to have someone on the team who can build new web pages as needed.

Recently I was talking to someone who had asked about the process for writing a book. While explaining it to them, I realized that I had used the same team for the manuscript editing, interior design and cover design for six books in total. (Catherine Leek of Green Onion Publishing does my editing and Kim Monteforte does my design work. Kim also designs all of my worksheets and templates for The Wealthy Speaker

School; you've seen a few samples of those inside this book and when you downloaded the PDFs on your Bonus Page.)

When you find someone good, you stick with them. Cathy, Kim and I have worked together for over a decade. There's a level of trust there that is worth every penny I spend with them.

We'll put links to all of my contractors in your Bonus Pages in case you need help in any of these areas.

BONUS PAGE

My Team: *www.speakerlauncher.com/scale*

Yikes! A well-paid job!! This had never dawned on me before.

The speaking business model isn't sustainable, salable or scalable unless you add revenue streams that are passive.

I really took this to heart and realized Dan was right. At that time, I was a coach. Like a speaker, basically, we have a calendar with slots to fill. You could fill 40 hours a week, and if you charged a good rate, you'd be doing pretty well. But you'd be limited. Also, if you've ever done any coaching, you may know that, mentally, 40 hours is really hard to do. Personally, I can't imagine coaching 40 hours a week – I'm tapped out at about half that. The point is, you will always have a limited amount of inventory. And that's no way to run a business, especially if you've ever thought about selling or scaling your business.

SUCCESS STORY
Ryan Estis

Moving to Multiple Millions

Let's use one of my clients, Ryan, a very busy, very popular keynoter as an example for speaking. Ryan delivers 70-80 keynotes in a normal year. He earns a whopping fee for each of those keynotes ($30K). But your fee and your calendar have limits. (We know that each speaking date often requires two additional days of travel.)

So, Ryan can earn a very healthy seven figures, but how high he can go into the millions will depend on what he earns off the stage, through product sales, courses, consulting (where a team is involved) or through investing.

I know you just did the math on that and thought, "Heck, I'll take it!" But what if you got sick? There's goes your income.

Up until recent years, when Ryan started to diversify and invest outside of speaking, he had an extremely well-paid job. But once he moved into passive income streams and developed income that didn't require him trading his time for money, he had a more solid, possibly even salable, business.

I realize that many of you reading this book would kill to have that type of revenue, but please see the limitations for scaling when you are trading your time for money.

Passive or Semi-Passive Income

So what are the options for bringing yourself in off the road and to stop trading so much of your time for money? Let's map them out and start to choose what's perfect for you. Perhaps you add just one, or over time add several, depending on your existing business model.

Here are my definitions for clarity.

- **Non-Passive Income:** A speech is a perfect example of *non*-passive income. Coaching is also non-passive. We are trading our time for money.
- **Passive or Semi-Passive Income:** The truth is, the term "passive" is misleading. By passive income, I am referring to revenue that does not require you to be involved full time. An online course is an example of passive income. But, as with most passive income streams, there is some set up on the front end and possibly some monthly effort to maintain the income.

We'll lay out some passive (semi-passive) income streams for you like a smorgasbord of options for you to choose from. We debated rating these on effort level, but there were too many variables. So, I hope you'll simply weigh your options and choose one or two to implement down the road. At the end of the chapter you'll find Exercise 12. It will help you explore all these options together in one spot.

Write a Book

Every time we write a new book, or add a revenue stream, it's like starting another small business. Even though some might think that writing a book is easy, there are many moving parts. A good chunk of time needs to be allotted to produce the book, but once you have it completed, a book can be leveraged in many ways.

The decision to self-publish or find an agent and sell to a publishing house deserves some thought. It's really going to depend on whether your purpose is to make money on the book. If a buck a book is your goal, then you might consider a publishing house. If you want to make \$5-\$10 per book, the self-publishing model is the way to go and, as a bonus, you retain control over many decisions, like the book's title, cover and content – it's all your branding and personality coming through. Some people want the caché of the publishing house and they want to use it to build their brand. This is not a bad plan when it comes to scaling, just do your homework and know all of the pros and cons before you sign anything.

Regardless of which direction, the steps remain the same. When you work with a professional, the editing moves from first draft, through developmental edit, content and copy editing. This may take several passes back and forth between author and editor and often a few months.

Then comes interior design – this is my favorite part because I'm such a visual person. A solid designer can capture your tone and style by using the right fonts and design.

Then of course there is printing if you decide to go the hard copy route. If you self-publish, be cautious with your early order numbers. Don't let the price breaks on printing 10,000 copies fool you. Someone needs to sell every one of those copies. Start low and build. Print-on-demand is a beautiful thing. Not as profitable, but saves your basement from storing boxes and boxes of books. (And trust me, I have had some very painful recycling moments, throwing out products that I never should have developed in the first place.)

Then, the real work begins when you start to promote the book. This is where big publishing houses have the ability to disappoint their authors. The expectation is often that they are going to put some money and talent behind the promotion of the book and some publishers are terrific. But just know that many of their ideas are going to involve work for you – it's a partnership. Although it does happen, it's rare to hear an author say, "The publisher did all the work. I just cashed the checks!"

The best way to sell books is through large audiences. Pre-selling the book when you get hired for a speech – getting a book into each attendee's hand – moves hundreds or thousands of copies at a time. If the client doesn't have it in their budget, perhaps they can find a sponsor who gets to be the hero when you say, "XYZ company has graciously purchased a copy of my book for each of you. I'll meet you at the back for an autograph session!" Followed by a big round of applause for XYZ!!!

Of course you can also sell your books back of the room (BOR), and that certainly helps to drive income. Many speakers can double their fee through product sales.

I think one of the biggest benefits of writing a book, and I may be preaching to the choir here, is that you now have all of your ideas down in a formula for success. Your thoughts have been documented. And guess what? You can use this content in many different ways. And that leads us to our next options.

Develop an Online Course

As with a book, there is an investment of effort and time up front – and infrastructure in this case – but an online course can definitely become a passive income stream. Especially if your program is "do it yourself" style, where people walk through it without any interaction with you. There are speakers who do quite well with this technique.

We opted for more of a hybrid version of our course. Sure, we can lay out the material for everybody, but people are going to have questions. Especially when our topic is so rich with different possibilities; there's really no "one size fits all" in The Wealthy Speaker School. Our hybrid version offers a course as well as a membership community. As a part of that package, we offer six or seven group coaching calls each month with different goals for each call. If you are looking for an entirely passive income stream, you are going to want to go with the stand-alone, do-it-yourself course.

The merits of combining course and community are engagement. Because our program involves a monthly fee, we strive to keep people not just for months, but for years as they grow through the stages of their business. And we have smaller groups, masterminds, for members to evolve into. I don't tell you this to encourage you to do the same. There are many, many moving parts and team members involved in my business model. Because of that many speakers would opt out of the hybrid model. I'm just laying out the options like a buffet. You can choose which pieces appeal to you.

When you develop your course, you'll need to figure out how big you want it. Amy Porterfield says that small, easy-to-consume courses are better. We opted to follow Brooke Castillo's strategy of giving more and more value in order to keep people in the School. It would take quite some time to pour through all of our lessons and we add more each month. But for a one-off course, you might consider Amy's idea of keeping it simple.

Give people enough to move the needle, but not so much that it kills you to produce the course.

There are a lot of course platforms or Learning Management Systems (LMS) out there – too many to name. One of the appealing features for me in originally choosing LearnDash was that it would allow people to mark their lessons complete once finished. We also have that feature in our new system Thinkific and I'm hoping people will be able to move around within the course even better. Figure out what features are really important to you and then shop around.

I know that Kajabi is popular with many and some even throw their programs up on Udemy. The Udemy strategy (hosting your course on a platform where you make peanuts but get a lot of exposure) is best, I think, for feeding one of your funnels. Say you have a short course on leadership inside Udemy, but that steers people to your paid mastermind group at a higher fee level and that then guides them into corporate work, which comes at a much higher dollar figure. You might see volume on Udemy but be aware that giving away something so cheap may not be in line with your brand.

Sometimes people think, "Oh, I'll just build an online course." In my experience, it's much easier said than done. If you decide to go this route, find someone who knows courses to help with the project and help you make decisions along the way. The biggest issue with your course will not be designing it, it will be selling it on an ongoing basis. You need a plan in place to do this.

SUCCESS STORY
Dr. Cindra Kamphoff

Combining Passive and Non-Passive Income

My client Cindra was thinking about how to diversify her income. She was a university professor, so had a busy "day job" but had been doing keynotes and workshops for years and was really seeing her brand explode. Her podcast, "High Performance Mindset," was also gaining traction. Cindra had a lot going for her, but wanted to scale, which meant creating some additional income streams.

To fill in her calendar slots between speeches, she took on executive coaching – this proved to be an income saver in the spring of 2020 when COVID-19 hit. But she also had an Academy that created passive income. She recruited people into her Academy from her live and virtual presentations. Her product sales, including her book, *Beyond Grit,* were doing very well – perhaps driven by her podcast. Cindra even went on to run a Mindset Summit where she brought together many of her peers for an additional revenue stream.

Today Cindra is a terrific example of balancing both passive and non-passive income.

How can you do a better job of combining both active and passive income?

Develop a Product Line

So, imagine you go into a company event and you relay your message of leadership. You have a through line in your presentation that everyone understands, digests and starts to use immediately. The line is "lead into the fire." The premise is that when the going gets tough, you don't shy away; you yell "bring it on!" because you're a strong leader.

The event goes swimmingly. When you return to the client's office six months later, you see your words "Lead into the Fire" everywhere!! They are on coffee mugs, motivational posters, screen savers, T-shirts and even Post-it® Notes. The client has purchased a copy of your book *Lead into the Fire* for everyone in the company. They took advantage of your product line to really sink your teachings into their culture. And you profited by doubling (or more) your speaking fee!

Wouldn't it be amazing if every company adopted your language/slogan/through line into their culture? That's one idea about a product line.

Here's another idea ...

Wouldn't it be amazing if people lined up at the back of the room to purchase all of your wares? Maybe you have books, workbooks, journals, T-shirts and mugs. If you can estimate your shipments, based on a certain percentage of the audience purchasing, then there is a lot to be said about BOR sales. It used to be the goal to, again, double the speaking fee with product sales. Of course, we need to be more creative during virtual or remote presentations to ensure that we don't forget to pitch our products.

Back of Room Sales

Back when I was representing Olympic athlete Vince, I booked several engagements for the direct selling company Amway. Each gig was in a stadium and we had anywhere from 15,000 to 24,000 people in the audiences. (I know, the glory days, right?) We knew product sales would be hot, so we developed an entire product line in four months in preparation for these events.

In those days, audio was "in" so we did two-packs of cassettes on several different topics. The bundle also included books and anything else we could think of. People lined up for three hours to get Vince's signature and purchase product. We took in anywhere from $10,000 to $25,000 in back-of-room product sales per engagement. I'll just say this. If you have a product, service or speech that can be promoted to the direct selling companies, then you may want to set your sights on that market. The people who show up to those events are pumped and ready to invest.

Vince was ready to capitalize on this opportunity. Doing a great job on the platform moved more product in those few engagements than we sold the entire rest of the year.

Personally, I don't love the idea of schlepping product but I do it when I speak because people want to take a piece of you home with them. They want to remember all that you talked about and, of course, your product line can help them go deeper. My goal during my session (typically a workshop for a group of speakers) is to sell them the dream. Typically, they want to spend money to capture that dream. And that's your goal as well when speaking. What's the dream that you're selling? Or the problem that you're fixing?

The idea of back of room is not entirely passive. But, if you are able to sell a lot of product from your website, and (like I do) have it shipped from a depot that manages the products for you, then you have true passive income.

This morning, I opened up my e-mail to orders that came in during the night. And the only "hands on" part of the transaction is moving the money into my bank account. Actually this happens automatically too, so I'm exaggerating. I don't do a darn thing!!!

Virtual Back of Room (BOR)

There is a lot of opportunity to convert virtual audiences into buyers. Are you taking advantage of virtual events to build your e-mail list or sell your products and online courses? There is business to be had from virtual presentations. Let's make sure we are asking for the sale.

What I love most about virtual is that you might mention your book, drive people to Amazon and then simply collect the check. Beautiful!!! Note: If you drive people to Amazon make sure that you have a way of grabbing their name and e-mail built into the book. (Like we do here in this book, with your Bonus Page.) When you sell books on Amazon you are missing out on building a relationship with this customer. Make sure that you have created a path that leads to you inside the book.

Perhaps you could give a copy of your book or eBook or seat in your course away during the presentation to attract attention to it. No doubt there are some fun ways to run a draw that would work for virtual presentations. A more subtle approach is to pull a quote or two from your book into your PowerPoint. Or you could read directly from your book. A special coupon for the book might entice people to buy right away. There are a lot of possibilities for selling BOR virtually.

Study Groups

Do you have a book or product that would do well with people forming study groups? We've all heard of Oprah's book club, but this idea is more specifically designed to help solve a problem. Perhaps your creations help people lose weight. Or let's say you have leadership products and services for black women – very niche topic. You might start a study group for one of your books called, *Black Women Leading*, and each member gets a copy of the book and study guide to follow. The group selects a leader who walks the class through the content. The fact that you don't need to run this yourself is brilliant and the benefit is that word spreads like wildfire.

Study groups could work for most every topic out there. When the book actually says, "Hey, be sure to check out our study guide and form your own class," you'll have groups popping up all over the world.

Create an App

The cost of designing an app used to be outrageous, but it's come down significantly over the years as more and more apps flood the market. Is your product or service app worthy?

One of mine was, but I didn't take the plunge. I have a really awesome product called *The Wealthy Speaker Daily Success Planner and Journal* that easily could have turned into an app. But I didn't have the bandwidth or the desire to flesh it out.

The best apps are ones that you need to use every day. Like "My Fitness Pal" for logging your daily food intake and exercise. One of my favorite apps has been "Win Streak" by Dan Sullivan. I've added Dan Sullivan's Win Streak app to your Bonus Page. It helps you focus on your "wins" every day. Every 24 hours at your allotted time, a reminder pops up on your phone and prompts you to record your wins. Doing this helps you build momentum.

Consulting/Advisory Work

Consulting work, at first blush, may not sound like a "passive" income stream. But there is a possibility where you could be the rainmaker, sell the project, and then lead the project, delegating the heavy lifting and details to the team or an outsourced party.

You could also have a company put you on retainer for a year or hire you as an advisor for a monthly fee. Often times, they don't require your services throughout the month, which then makes the income from that month "passive."

I'm not an expert on consulting but I do have expertise on building a business that's perfect for you and what's possible! Sometimes when you are up to your neck in client work, it's really hard to see what's possible.

The goal is that you take on only the pieces of the project that you love, not all of the nitty-gritty things that you aren't wild about. Perhaps there are some measurements that need to be taken to help you gauge results of your consulting work. You might see if the company can perform those internally and then you work with the raw data. Or you outsource the measurement work.

I can hear you now, "But my clients trust me. They need *me*." As long as the work gets done and your outcomes are the same, will they be concerned with how it happened? You making yourself indispensable to your clients might feel good, but it doesn't lead to scaling. Be indispensable as the expert with the solutions, the leader of the deliverables, not the person doing the grunt work.

Offering a Wide Range of Consulting

I asked my friend Randy if I could show a list of the types of projects that he'd do inside his consulting company. As you can see the majority of his work is in the "culture" space. His role is helping the following:

- A middle-market food manufacturing client to create a high-performance culture that contributed to seeing their revenue double in 15 months while also being named a "Best Place to Work" in the Denver area.
- A middle-market electronic manufacturing client that was formed from the merger of two independent companies, with locations on the east coast, Silicon Valley, and China, to create a shared vision, build a high-performing organization and create a unified culture.
- An independent school district to create the portrait of a successful high school graduate in the year 2035 and then assist the leadership in creating a culture and organization that can achieve that goal.
- A national not-for-profit to foster a culture of collaboration and co-creation within its national office and local members to achieve its mission.
- A $280 million regional operation for a multi-billion-dollar food industry client to create a high-performing culture that meets customer expectations, maintains high morale and increases profit margins.

As you can see consulting gives you a wide variety of day-to-day work. This sure doesn't look like you'd get bored! I asked Randy about whether or not he completes all of the tasks himself. Here's what he said:

> I do all of the strategy and high-level work myself. I bring in a second pair of hands to do qualitative and quantitative research when needed, and I will occasionally use others to do some of the training. More and more these days, I create the train-the-trainer material to equip the client with the ability to deliver

> on-going training for everything below the executive and department manager levels. That saves them money and creates buy-in to continue to use the material.
>
> My research person is a brand-planning expert with about 30 years of experience. She works with lots of big companies to understand the voice of the customer.
>
> Interestingly, I used to use contract resources more than I do these days. I find that one of the key selling points is that they get me, not someone supervised by me.

I'm sure Randy and I could have a spirited debate about whether or not he needs to sell the client on him doing the work, but really I just love showing you that there is no one "right" way.

Consulting may not be for everybody. There is a ton of work and time that goes into the types of projects that Randy offers his clients in order to get these incredible deliverables.

Start a Membership Community

Here's a revenue stream that is a bit more passive – but not entirely!

A membership community is one where people pay you monthly or annually to participate in your work and help them solve a problem. My School is where speakers come to "build the business of their dreams." Through our courses we teach them how to do it. But the community is what inspires action. People join the calls to get inspired, get new ideas and continue to move their business forward.

Depending on how busy you are with speaking, you may put a community coordinator in place. I have Jen, a graduate of my program, who's been with me for over five years delivering the bulk of the work within the School, freeing me up to do work at the masters level. My involvement is two calls per month. But, I also help sell the School, lead the team and develop new content.

Permit me a little side note here. When looking for people to hire, search within your audiences for people who love what you do and want to be a part of it. (Refer back to Strategy #5 on hiring.)

I don't want you to take the launch of a community lightly. You might be able to get people signed up fairly easily, but keeping them there is when the heavy lifting comes into play. You need to be developing content and engagement throughout any given month in order to see your community grow.

> ***Getting people into your community might be easy, but getting them to stay takes engagement!***

The person who I know to be the expert on membership is Stu McLaren. Check out his website at stu.me; there's always a freebie you can grab to give you some of the basics.

Running Your Membership

My client Michelle, a "retired" doctor with expertise in mindful eating, runs a membership program called the "Mindful Eating Support Community." It is for people who want to break their eat-repent-repeat cycle, heal their relationship with food and their body, and live the vibrant life they crave. (A program that many of us, including myself, could use!)

She offers three levels for her program. There are a lot of moving parts so I'm going to spell them out so you can consider what you might want for your membership.

- The highest level, called Commitment, includes coaching with Michelle's trained coaches. Michelle has licensed more than 700 health and wellness professionals, including coaches, to offer her work – another fabulous way to scale your business.
- Her middle level, Connected, is for people new to the program or people who need a refresher on the content.

- And her Continuing level is for folks who have been through the program and want to keep going. This is where many online courses fail. They leave people at the finish line with nowhere else to go.

Depending on what level of investment they've made, Michelle's members gain access to a number of features like:

- private Facebook community moderated by Michelle,
- monthly skill-building webinar (recording available for three months),
- choice of three mindful eating courses,
- monthly group coaching session on Zoom,
- discounts on products and services, and
- private coaching (in highest level).

Michelle loves to leverage her time! Her "Mindful Eating Programs" were recorded during a live paid webinar series and are also used in her online training programs. The monthly skill-building webinars are also provided to her licensees to watch for a month as a value-add. As well, she put together a package of the PowerPoint slides, handouts and recordings that her licensees can purchase to offer workshops or webinars in their companies or for their clients.

Michelle has a lot going on in her business, but if you'll look closely, once she has launched a program, there's not a lot of additional work for her as the content is already in place and ready to go.

Start a Mastermind Group

Years ago, one of my clients told me that she would pay more to be in a smaller group of people who would receive coaching from me. It was right about that time that people paying for masterminds started to take off. So we took advantage and started the Inner Circle Mastermind over a decade ago. A year-long program for speakers who wanted to scale – most were aiming for seven figures.

At first we met once per month, but I realized quickly that wasn't frequent enough. So we moved it to twice per month. I included quarterly coaching with me in the package to really sweeten the pot. Today, all of our Inner Circle members also get full access to the School, which is a huge bonus. A part of our mastermind offering has also been to allow the group to meet and bond in person through our live events. For many years we have run live events and are currently re-examining those to possibly be replaced by a Virtual Summit. The jury is still out on that one.

If you are a leadership expert, then I would think you'll be helping leaders build trust and influence with their team over a period of time following your formula.

Once you decide on the outcome and the curriculum, then think about the delivery. Do you want to meet weekly for a short period of time, or twice per month for a year? This is your party, do it in a way that is perfect for you, your skills and your schedule.

The outcome is that you launch groups like this several times per year and boost your revenue from masterminds. Another step in scaling.

SUCCESS STORY

Ozan Varol

Creating a Mastermind that Works

My client Ozan, a rocket scientist by trade, has created several levels of masterminds. Much of his success started with his book, *Think Like a Rocket Scientist*. When that book got chosen as one of Amazon's Best Books of the Year, his brand got another bump.

Another rainmaker for his income streams is his newsletter. *The Contrarian* has over 25,000 subscribers (likely more at the time of this printing). Every week he offers one big idea that readers can digest in under three minutes. And that helps feed his mastermind.

His Inner Circle Mastermind is a lower-fee program that allows his clients to peek inside his world through master classes, live coaching and a private community.

He also has an upgraded version called Moonshot Mastermind at a much higher price point. It's designed for high caliber leaders who have set big goals for their businesses. Where his lower fee group may have hundreds or thousands of members, the smaller, more exclusive groups (six to ten people) gain direct access to Ozan's brain. And they also create a much deeper set of results. And a fun twist? Ozan's wife, Kathy (who has 20 years of experience in strategy, impact and brand marketing), runs the program alongside him.

Coaching (Non-Passive)

Building a coaching calendar around your speaking schedule takes work but is doable. Although not passive income, it's a nice way to shore up your finances when any manner of calamity strikes! And it's a great way to fill in holes in your calendar.

My client Cindra, who I mentioned earlier, is a psychologist and mental performance expert. She was having a banner year in speaking, but around the beginning of 2020 she expressed her desire to increase her executive coaching clients. Well, low and behold, she had just secured several new clients when COVID-19 hit and all of her speaking engagements got bounced. Her executive coaching helped her stay on track with her revenue goals during the worst part of the economic slump.

I have several clients who are coaches and their background and experience make them perfect for the job; they didn't need any extra training. The question about whether to become certified or not is one that you could ask ten people and get ten different answers. I can just speak for myself.

I've been trained as a coach (by Coaches Training Institute) but did not get certified. Nor did I feel the need since my coaching slides so far into the consulting realm. (People pay me for answers – that's somewhat different from the straight up coaching model). I will, however, become certified in Brooke Castillo's Thought Model program because I want to grow from the process as much as have another powerful tool for my clients.

I'm going to assume that because you have a level of expertise in a specific area, that you are qualified to coach around that area. But you'll know whether or not additional training is required.

Follow-Up Series

You have a client who has a problem. A single presentation might feel like you're putting a Band-Aid™ on a gaping wound. So, how do you continue to see results long after your presentation is over?

Perhaps you develop a video series that allows your audience to hang out with you on a regular basis. You launch the idea at the keynote or main event, and then they get one video message from you each week (or month or quarter), depending on how you think the content would be best received.

The beauty of a package like this is that once you develop it, you can offer to all clients. (You may make it exclusive to one industry at a time if your client requests it.)

If video isn't your thing, then maybe those follow-ups are with you in person or virtually? What's perfect for you? With Zoom being so easy and widely accepted, perhaps you offer a monthly or quarterly Zoom call with you to answer questions and keep the message alive. Make sure you name these calls something interesting. "Monthly Revenue Builder" would be a call that I'd want to attend, wouldn't you?

You could also build coaching or executive coaching in as a follow-up option.

How to Go Deeper with Your Message

My client Brittany talks about how to make Superfans of your customers. She has a stronghold in the financial services space with her most requested keynote, "Creating Superfans," which shares a five-part game plan for taking potential customers from apathy to advocacy. She uses the acronym SUPER to cover five important components of sales, marketing and customer experience.

When one of her clients asked how they could dive deeper into her message, they brainstormed and landed on a series of five follow-up videos delivered by Brittany. By drilling down on her keynote, she created five additional hours of deep-dive content (one hour for each part of her SUPER game plan) to help her client's employees hit the ground running with implementation.

Brittany also developed a playbook that the leader of the meeting could use to keep the conversations on track.

Not only does the message run deep, the results are fantastic for Brittany's client and they will want to do the same year after year. Plus, Brittany can now sell the follow-up series and playbook as an add-on to her keynote. Beyond the inspiring stage delivery, clients have a rock-solid plan for empowering their employees to create real change in the weeks and months after the live event. How does this position Brittany as the go-to hero for customer experience with her clients? You guessed it, she's cementing loyalty and creating her own Superfans.

Live Events (Non-Passive)

Live events are a terrific way to bring your people to you. This is definitely not passive income. Live events may be the most work of any of these ideas (perhaps competing with online courses).

SUCCESS STORY Dan Miller

Bringing Your People to You!

Dan, author of *48 Days to the Work You Love,* lives in Tennessee on a beautiful ranch and brings groups of people to him – many at a time. Brilliant!

Dan decided early in his speaking business that the travel should be done only for cherry picked (rainmaking) events and the rest of the audiences he would bring to him. When you've got that kind of trust built in with your audience, switching over to virtual – which Dan already did as a part of his programming – is not that big of a leap.

Dan's business model also includes:

- retreats,
- rallies,
- multi-day trainings or conferences,
- day-long events,
- half-day teasers and
- virtual conferences, trainings or summits (longer in format).

Think about the Tony Robbins model. The goal would be to get you to a one- or two-day event (teaser) at a big venue at a reasonable price. This would cement your loyalty in for longer and more expensive training and coaching down the road. They were selling the dream and selling it hard. The last time I attended, the pot of gold was a live event in Hawaii at the highest price point.

The way they moved you from one price point to another was masterful. Nobody does live events like Tony Robbins!

And you should check out the YouTube of his virtual events on your Bonus Page. He was one of the first to deliver a live event format with thousands of attendees on the screens around him. Very cool!

BONUS PAGE

Tony Robbins YouTube: *www.speakerlauncher.com/scale*

• • •

So, we've laid out a few options for you in terms of income streams. Exercise 12 will help you explore all these different revenue streams. No doubt there are more ideas that you might find and implement. What we want to do is find things that match your strengths and implement those. And it may be a combination of a couple of things that really makes the income needle move.

Exercise 12:

WHICH REVENUE STREAMS DO YOU LOVE?

Now is the time to start running your business, instead of it running you. You'll find questions under each of the different revenue streams below. Discover which are a good fit for your business, will help you scale and that you'll enjoy!

Writing a Book

Here are some questions that will help you decide if writing a book is for you. There are more questions you can ask yourself, but these will help get you started.

1. Do you want to self-publish or go with a publisher?

____

____

____

2. Who is your target audience for this book?

____

____

____

3. What's the main problem you want to solve?

____

____

____

4. Do you have an audience already in place waiting to purchase (database, live or virtual audiences)?

____

____

____

5. How will you promote and sell your book?

____

____

____

Online Course

Creating an online course is a terrific step towards creating passive income. Here are some questions to consider.

1. Who is your online course for?

____

____

____

2. What problem will your course solve?

____

____

____

3. Do you have an audience ready and waiting to buy your course (database, live or virtual audiences)?

____

____

____

4. How will you promote your online course?

____

____

____

Spread Your Message with Products

These questions will help you determine if a product line will work for you.

1. What types of products are in the running (a possible product you'd like to carry) and are not on your list? (Examples: "yes" to a T-shirt (light, easy to ship); "no" to a poster (tricky to transport).)

____

____

____

2. Once you have your yes/no list, what products might you build a combo package from?

____

____

____

3. Do you have built-in audiences ready and waiting for your products (database, live or virtual events)?

____

____

____

Virtual BOR

Don't forget to sell your products during virtual events too.

1. What are you doing to sell product during your virtual presentations?

____

____

____

2. How can you drive people to your website?

____

____

____

3. How will you collect names and e-mail addresses?

____

____

____

Study Group as Product

Here are a few questions to guide you along the study group option.

1. Do you have a product that would go nicely with study groups? If not, can it be tweaked to work? How?

____

____

____

2. Do you have followers (evangelists) that would hop on this idea right away?

____

____

____

Morphing a Product into an App

If you think you have an app-worthy product or service, consider these questions to get started.

1. Do you have an idea for an app?

____

____

____

2. Can you develop this yourself or can someone on your team? Or do you need to contract this out?

____

____

____

3. Do you have an audience who would want the app?

____

____

____

4. How will you sell this app on an ongoing basis?

____

____

____

Making Consulting Passive – for You

If you think consulting might be for you, work through these questions to get your answer.

1. What aspects of consulting work make you happy?

____

____

____

2. Which parts of the consulting work do you want to farm out?

____

____

____

3. Who do you have on your team or in your inner circle who might help you?

____

4. How do you shift from selling speeches (one-offs) to solutions (consulting packages)?

Building a Membership Community

Explore these questions to decide if a membership community would work to scale your business.

1. Do you have the bandwidth to start a membership community?

2. Are you prepared to pull people into these groups? Who will those people be?

3. What outcome will you provide? What problem will you solve?

4. Do you have ideas on how to continuously engage and keep your members happily involved?

____

____

____

Mastermind Groups for Ultimate Scaling

Review these questions to determine if a mastermind group fits your strategy.

1. What does your perfect offering look like? (How long is it, how often will you meet, etc.?)

____

____

____

2. What outcome do you want to offer? What problem will you help solve?

____

____

____

3. How can you create solid results for your mastermind clients?

____

____

____

Coaching – Not Passive But Reliable

When you set up a coaching practice, you want to check off a few considerations.

Yes	No	
☐	☐	Is coaching for me?
☐	☐	Do you have enough experience to coach people legitimately?
☐	☐	Do you have the skill set to move your clients through a problem?

If you answered "no" to either of the last two questions, then you might seek some coaching training to make sure that you have some foundations in place.

Follow-Up Offering

If you think following up your speaking gig with coaching or executive coaching might be an option for scaling your business, start with these questions.

1. Is a follow-up program for me?

   ____

   ____

   ____

2. Which type of follow-up program suits you best (video, coaching, webinars, etc.)?

   ____

   ____

   ____

3. What steps are involved in starting it?

____

____

____

Live Events – The Not So Passive Income

So what's perfect for you? Perhaps you don't want to travel and bringing people to your backyard works. Or maybe you love traveling to exotic locations, so being with a group there makes sense. Perhaps you want to fill your own classroom right next door.

Here are some things to think about.

1. Are live events for you? (Remember, a lot of planning goes into a live event.)

____

____

____

2. Who will help with logistics and all of the details of a live event?

____

____

____

3. Selling live events (putting bums in seats) is hard. Who is going to sell it and how?

____

____

____

4. Do you have a database that you can market these events to? Are they willing to buy?

____

____

____

Just remember, you need a system to implement your launches of whatever products and services you choose so that you have some predictability within your marketing calendar. If your team knows that every February you run your live event and every October you launch your mastermind, then they can be prepared for those ahead of time.

Whether it be adding more passive income or adding more active income streams – you'll be glad to expand your revenue.

Strategy #7

Develop Your Virtual Speaking Strategy

Booking More Virtual Work

At the time of writing *Scaling Your Speaking Business*, we had been dealing with the fallout of COVID-19 for what felt like ages. In fact, I was tired of even talking about it. I hope that by the time you are laying eyes on this book that the virus is in our rear-view mirror. That said, I think our new reality is that virtual is here to stay and, personally, I believe that's a good thing for my clients. Why? Because it gives you options.

You can go out on the road speaking for as many dates as *you* want (pandemic or other catastrophe pending) because you can supplement your live presentations with virtual work. Sure, we know that there's nothing like the energy of a live audience, but virtual allows you to:

- make money while in your slippers (sleeping in your own bed at night);
- lower your number of travel days each year (perhaps leading to a healthier lifestyle);
- fill in gaps in your calendar;
- deliver multiple engagements in a day (easily); and
- help clients in ways that we've never thought of before.

How cool is that???

In fact, I believe so strongly in the benefits of virtual presentations that I created a webinar on Building Your Virtual Speaking Business. Check out your Bonus Page.

BONUS PAGE

Building Your Virtual Speaking Business:
www.speakerlauncher.com/scale

If you have yet to embrace virtual work, then that's your prerogative, but I think it's here to stay so we might as well welcome the opportunity. Those on my client roster who have embraced it have done it with such zest that it's really been a game changer in their business.

SUCCESS STORY

Pamela Barnum

Embracing Virtual

Let me brag for a minute on my mastermind client Pamela, a body language and trust expert. In the beginning of the 2020 pandemic, she said, during a mastermind session, something that many of you might have thought, "I hate virtual!"

With the thought model being so top of mind for me, I simply asked, "Do you really?" She quickly recognized that she really needed to change up her thinking about it, which she proceeded to do. And guess what? Not only did virtual work start flowing in the doors of Pamela's business, she put together a studio and the technology to really thrive in it.

After doing several remote events that were exceptionally well received, a speakers bureau approached her and asked her to deliver training on how to build trust during virtual presentations. She moved from "I hate virtual" to being so good at it that people were asking her how she did it!

We'll put a link to a session we did with Pamela about how to deliver engaging virtual presentations on your Bonus Page.

BONUS PAGE

Virtual Presentations: *www.speakerlauncher.com/scale*

Delivery Options for Virtual

Let's think about all of the options for how to deliver virtually, and then I want to get to the fun part – the money! Most of you will already have this down, but perhaps there's one idea or tweak that you can take advantage of.

What are our options when it comes to delivery?

- **Workshops and webinars (sit down sessions).** There are so many ways to deliver your content. You can have a PowerPoint heavy message, with you in the top corner of the screen. It can be all you on the screen, just moving through your material. You can be engaging the audience and taking questions the entire time or you can hold Q&A until the end. Trial and error will allow you to see how you can deliver workshops and webinars that best fit your skill set and content.
- **Keynotes (in-house, stand-up sessions**). When you are tasked to deliver a keynote, my belief is that the energy is higher when you are standing and moving around. Now some people have a ton of technology going on all around them and that makes up the difference for not standing – find what works for you. Some of your keynotes will be pre-recorded and some will be live. If the client has a solid budget, a pre-recorded keynote might even have you moving the session from your home office to a local studio.
- **Keynotes (in-studio, stand-up sessions).** For those of you who have built the studio in your home, well done! You have really embraced the virtual idea and I think it will serve you in the long run. If that's not the case, perhaps there's a studio that is set and

ready to go in your hometown. Imagine driving 20 minutes and working with professionals to lock down an awesome recording of your presentation. That feels pretty good as well. And the clients who want all of the bells and whistles know that they need to foot the bill, so turning them on to your local studio as an option is a win-win. You can build the studio fee into your pricing or have the client book it directly.

Pivoting Towards Opportunity

One of my best friends in the industry is Kris. She worked for years inside a speaker bureau, then moved to event production companies. At the beginning of 2020, she landed a role with a Minneapolis-based (her hometown) company, Heroic Productions, as VP of Speakers & Entertainment.

Kris's new job was to book speakers and entertainment into the live events that her company produced. You know these people – they work the sound board at the back of the room, wear the headsets, operate the cameras, install the IMAG screens, etc. Those are the production companies.

Two weeks into Kris's new gig and COVID hit! And live events went away! Fortunately, Heroic Productions was nimble. As luck would have it, they had just taken over an entire building with office and warehouse space. One of the warehouse spaces was empty. As gear and crew came back in off the road, they immediately went to work building a broadcast studio, with three beautiful stages, each with LED backdrops and one huge green screen.

Overnight their business changed. Instead of hauling gear and crew to live events all over the country, clients were now coming to them to create high quality, pre-recorded and/or live-streamed events (in-studio or completely virtual).

Kris's company stayed focused on the needs of their clients during a difficult time. This allowed them to pivot very quickly into the new virtual world. You know the saying, "Success happens when preparation meets opportunity." They focused on the client and how their needs changed. The more quickly you can shift to meet those needs, the more quickly you'll be able to grow and scale.

Here's a little side note. Kris's personal pivot was just as dramatic. In early 2020, her clients weren't thinking about hiring speakers right away. They had to get their brains around shifting events to virtual. In most cases, the events were really scaled back (essentials only). Kris started consulting with clients about the virtual capabilities her company offered, and her 30 years of consulting on content and speakers paid off handsomely. Kris learned that the planning process for virtual was exactly the same – only more work! Speaker bookings came back quickly and she was able to help her clients plug the right talent into the right spot on the virtual conference agenda.

One thing is for sure, virtual is here to stay and those who pivoted were ready to take on the opportunity.

Can I Get Paid Well for Virtual?

I'd like to answer this question with a resounding, "Heck yeah!" You can get paid for virtual. Of course, there was confusion within companies around budgets for virtual in the spring and summer of 2020, the beginning of the pandemic; we were all roaming around in the Wild West of business back then.

I suspect when people weren't given good budgets, they hired hacks instead of professional speakers and experts, and a lot of meetings bombed because they weren't dealing with pros. But, the budgets have been coming back and we continue to see bigger more beautifully produced events designed to engage the home viewer.

I heard a statistic that of the $800 billion (yes that's a "b") that would be spent in the meeting industry in the year of COVID-19, 80% of that would still be in play. At this time, I can only speculate that budgets for virtual meetings will continue to grow as companies witness the power of using awesome technology combined with professional talent (speakers and experts). And once the pandemic is behind us, we'll continue to see hybrid meetings with a combination of live and virtual.

Moving from Transaction to Transformation

When a client calls, they are likely trying to fill a spot. "Are you free on such-and-such a date for a this-or-that virtual event?" So it's easy to be lured down the road of transaction. "Yes, I'll come and do your virtual event for my price." But don't let that be the scope of your work with this client. Start by asking questions. Exercise 13 will help you get started moving from transaction (one presentation) to transformation (a package of services).

Exercise 13:
MAKE VIRTUAL EVENTS TRANSFORMATIONAL

Just because a session is virtual doesn't mean it can't be more. You can move past the event planner's expectations and bring transformation to the organization, just as you would for any other gig.

1. What does the organization want to accomplish with this event?

 ____

 ____

 ____

2. What would your role be?

 ____

____

____

3. How long do they want your message to last – are they thinking of a transformational change?

____

____

____

4. What's going on in their organization?

____

____

____

When you hit question four in Exercise 13, you're now starting to move towards providing a solution to their problem. Imagine the goal for the annual meeting of ABC company is to strive for more diversity and inclusion. Well, a 45-minute presentation by you, an expert in D&I, may start some conversation flowing, but is that the end? Perhaps you make some recommendations that will go beyond this one event, and allow them to follow through on their initiative in a more meaningful manner.

Now we're moving towards transformation.

And transformation comes in packages.

The Package Versus the One-Off

Okay, so your client would like to see some serious change happen in ABC company's culture when it comes to diversity, inclusion and all-around kindness in their workplace. Okay, what can your role in this process be and how might that look?

Perhaps the keynote on the date they enquired about is only the first step. But then there's a follow-up deep dive Q&A session afterwards. Perhaps there's a series of workshops to expand on your materials that happen over four weeks or four months? Maybe you consult with them to help really drive the messages home or do some executive coaching with the team. There are many ways for you to be helpful for your audiences. I really hope you are able to engage them in meaningful conversations so that you can make the recommendations necessary to truly effect change.

But that feels self-serving.

Does it really feel self-serving if you are helping a company transform? Really? Gosh, I hope not. We have the opportunity to come at this from a place of service. My good friend Chris West suggests that you show up to a meeting with curiosity leading your thoughts rather than, "Geez, I hope I make a sale." Being curious and asking good questions will really allow you to unearth the needs of the client and make recommendations.

BONUS PAGE

Increasing Your Virtual Bookings with Chris West:
www.speakerlauncher.com/scale

Check out the podcast I did with Chris West on the subject of Increasing Your Virtual Bookings on your Bonus Page.

Strategy #8

Develop Systems for Booking More Live Events

Many of you, as intermediate or seasoned speakers, have systems in place to bring in the business.

You've decided ahead of time what your strategy is going to be and set about implementing it. If you feel as though your sales funnels are strong, congratulations! You've already achieved one of the toughest pieces of the puzzle in the speaking business. But what about when it comes to growth?

Let's check in on your systems and see if there is anything we might add either to scale or to move you closer to the "working smarter not harder" mode.

We can break it down into two main areas.

1. Passive outbound marketing – frequent and steady marketing that builds your brand and awareness.
2. Selling direct – the call-send-call approach to outbound sales calls and e-mails designed to book business directly.

Passive Outbound Marketing

Creating systems that put you in front of your buyers on a regular basis is a terrific way to build your brand, your expertise and your business.

You can do this by placing very focused content out to the target markets that you want to be known in.

Beware the Content "Rabbit Holes"

Now let me say a little more about focused content. When you are delivering your thoughts to your followers, your fan base and your prospects – whether it be through your blog, videos or social media posts – be aware of when you are going down a rabbit hole that leads to nowhere.

When you fill your channels with all kinds of topics, just because you're interested in them, you may be doing your brand a disservice. I'm talking about the productivity expert who writes blog posts about teambuilding with no link back to productivity. It's the sales expert who shoots a video on employee engagement. You should be talking and writing about your expertise 90% of the time.

One of my clients, who shall remain nameless ☺, is quite famous for getting into arguments on social media. He weighs in on everything – not just the big social injustice battles, I mean *everything*. And because of that, I wonder if clients who vet their speakers thoroughly via their social footprint could be turned off. So pick your battles. If you see something that you just can't let pass, then go for it. But if you weigh in on everything, you must know that this is going to impact your business.

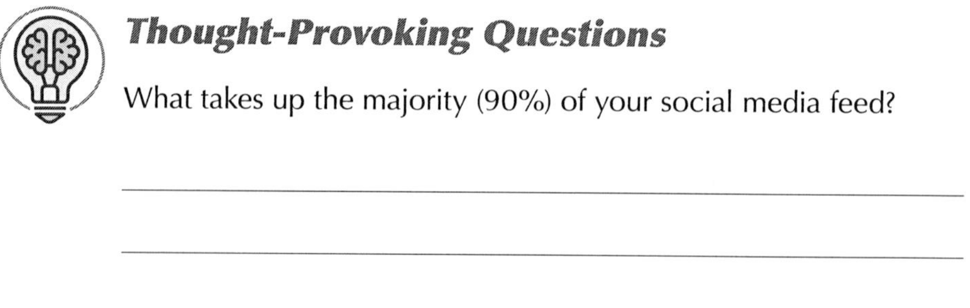

Thought-Provoking Questions

What takes up the majority (90%) of your social media feed?

What subjects will you steer clear of?

___

___

___

What subjects will you brave it out and state your opinion on?

___

___

___

I've wanted to write about topics off brand on my blog – in fact, I wrote an entire book about love and relationships. It did not support my brand one bit and was a big mistake. I cannot tell you how many times I have wanted to scream on social media about a topic that I know is polarizing (like politics, which I feel very passionate about). I have had to resist. Number one, it's not worth arguing with people who don't hold the same views as you – trust me you will never change anyone's mind – and, number two, it may be hurting your brand. You have to decide if it's worth it.

Finding Your Marketing Superpower

Without commitment to a schedule, marketing can be like throwing spaghetti at a wall to see what sticks.

So, if we agree that you're going to put out quality information about your expertise, the next step is to figure out how you want to relay that content. Creating the right passive outbound system means really checking in with what you are good at in terms of delivery. Are you a rock star at video? Are you a great writer? Do your social media posts capture a lot of attention?

Figure out what you love and what you are good at. Then build a schedule and commit to that.

Meridith Powell is great on video. She consistently puts out "Business Growth Tips" on video that allow her clients (business owners and leaders) to see her as the answer to their problems.

Ozan Varol is a great writer. He publishes a newsletter called *The Contrarian* every Thursday that goes to his 20,000+ followers.

Kindra Hall sees a cumulative effect from her client e-mails, video and social media posts, and her book. She believes her success comes down to consistency across the board.

Ryan Estis puts out a newsletter every Sunday called *Prepare for Impact* that his readers love.

Doug Sandler became a superstar with his "Nice Guys on Business" podcast. Podcasting became his way of feeding his funnel and a new business focus.

So, if you don't already have a marketing calendar that is operating like a well-oiled machine, intentionally pumping out content around your expertise, that may be something you need to get in place in order to scale.

SUCCESS STORY
Doug Sandler

Finding Your Superpower

Doug came to me for coaching because he wanted to grow his speaking business. Having run a very successful DJ business in DC, Doug started his brand "Nice Guys" and wrote the book *Nice Guys Finish First*. When he launched his podcast "Nice Guys on Business," his superpower took hold and he quickly realized that he was able to monetize in different ways than he originally thought.

His podcast was so successful that everybody kept asking him for advice. And, being a nice guy, he would share. Doug realized that his passion was in podcasts. Sure, speaking was going to be a part of his strategy – as a rainmaker for his other income streams – but he moved many of his efforts towards being a coach and consultant in podcasting and started a company that helps podcasters produce and deliver quality material. I can say "quality" easily, because I'm a client of Turnkey Podcasts and they do an amazing job.

We'll put a link to a podcast I did with Doug on your Bonus Page.

BONUS PAGE

The Power of Podcasts with Doug Sandler:
www.speakerlauncher.com/scale

Sometimes our superpower doesn't end up being what we expected, but when you find it, it feels easy, it feels like a fit and you are able to consistently create content without a lot of drama or stress. To hone in on your superpowers, try Exercise 14.

Exercise 14:

FOCUSING YOUR SUPERPOWERS

Your superpower may have you doing any of the following as a part of your passive outbound marketing strategy.

Marketing Initiatives	Yes	Frequency Commitment
Newsletter	☐	______
Blog Post	☐	______
Guest Blogger	☐	______
Podcast	☐	______
Podcast Guest	☐	______

Webinars	☐	________
Social Media	☐	________
Video	☐	________
Asking for Referrals	☐	________
Paid Advertising (Google, Facebook, Instagram, etc.)	☐	________
Media (TV, print, radio)	☐	________
Contests/Giveaways	☐	________
Article Placement	☐	________
Other	☐	________

Batching Your Work

The marketing machine is what allows you to work smarter not harder. And remember, your part in this should be relatively small, provided you are not caught up in perfectionism.

For instance, when I put together a blog post, there are several hours of work involved in the steps. Writing is my part, which takes 30-40 minutes but then it gets passed off to the team. They edit it, make it sound good, make it look good (add graphics and pictures), write up the teaser for it, which is sent in the form of an e-mail, and publish it to the blog.

Writing a piece of content can take minutes or hours – it's all going to come down to team and trust.

My role was that first 30-40 minutes – and that's it.

If I block off three hours, I can pump out three to four posts in one sitting.

The same goes with video. My team and I put together one-minute videos to go out as #Speaker SuccessTips that we can use on social media and e-mail marketing – you gotta love double dipping, using content several different ways. When I'm not filming, I'm creating a list of ideas for the tips. Because they are only one minute in length, I can sit down for 30 minutes and film a bunch of them all at once.

We also have the same approach of batching with our podcast. We record only on Mondays, typically no more than three in a sitting. I know some people who record ten in one day. That wouldn't work for me; I get tapped out more quickly. When you find your magic number, go with it!

Social media may be where you'll feel the most push back when it comes to delegating. Many people want social media to be in their voice. So you have the team batch it up and you run through it to see what they have planned. Once you get into the groove with your team, they will come up with ideas that you would never have thought of, and your content is still at the core.

Think about how much time you spend on social media each day and whether or not this is a good use of your time. We've all been down that rabbit hole only to find ourselves one or two hours later thinking, "What just happened?!" That's why dealing with social media in batches (by someone else) is so much more effective. They schedule it up and then you can designate 15-30 minutes a day on responses to notifications. And of course, beware of rabbit holes and videos of bulldogs on skateboards, the supreme wasters of time!

And when you have the right team members in place to take your work and make it better, then you truly are working smarter not harder.

Blocking off chunks of time to "batch" your work really helps you feel in control of your business. Exercise 15 will help you sort through this practice.

If you are still editing your writing, or adding logos to your videos, or posting to your blog, you may have difficultly scaling since your time is being spent doing the $30/hour jobs. Be careful that being a control freak or perfectionist doesn't get in the way of what you desire long term. Done is better than perfect.

I found a good quote about this, but not sure who wrote it, "When you try to control everything, you enjoy nothing."

Exercise 15:
BATCH YOUR WORK

Sending focused content out to your targeted markets often and in a consistent way fosters brand awareness, sets you up as an expert and scales your business. Here are some questions that will allow you to move this idea forward.

1. What is your marketing superpower (writing, video, social media, PR)? You might draw from Exercise 14 to answer this question.

   ____

   ____

   ____

2. How can you batch your work to make it easier?

   ____

   ____

   ____

3. Who should be doing each part of the process? (Hint: it's not you!)

   ____

   ____

   ____

Dan Sullivan has a new book out called *Who Not How* (available October 2020 – check your Bonus Page for a link) that focuses on asking "Who can do this for me?"

BONUS PAGE

Dan Sullivan, *Who Not How*: *www.speakerlauncher.com/scale*

So now that we have your passive outbound marketing sorted, let's move into a more targeted approach for getting booked for speeches and other revenue streams.

Selling Direct

Our second possible approach is more specifically focused. Selling direct is identifying opportunities and selling into them. Whether you are selling consulting packages, speeches or training, there is usually a similar path to follow.

1. Identify target markets that need your service.
2. Put together a hit list of prospects.
3. Reach out (via e-mail, phone, social media) to assess whether or not there is a need.
4. Follow up through to close.

That may sound overly simplified, but once you get into the rhythm of the four steps, you can rinse and repeat as often as needed. Some people will have a continuous stream of leads going into the hopper and will never let up on their sales effort. While others will work mainly through spin off (additional business produced from the original gig) once their marketing machine has produced enough business. Whether or not there will be enough spin off to maintain you depends on how many engagements you want to deliver each year.

When a pandemic, economic downturn or natural disaster hits and all of your business gets pushed out into the future, that spin-off business isn't there. So what do we do? Many business owners circle back to what worked in the early days.

In year one, you are hungry and you are calling and e-mailing everyone you know. You're out hustling for the business. And I think this can always work, even in a time of crisis, with one caveat – that you are coming from a place of service rather than desperation. Your stance or approach when talking to customers should always be one of curiosity (like my friend Chris West says) rather than "I could really use this sale." Be aware of how you are coming at sales in any situation and that you are coming from a place of confidence and abundance.

Business as a Numbers Game

You might have thought about your business as a blank farmer's field when you were first starting out. You went out and you planted seeds, fertilized and then saw a harvest. But you likely didn't stop planting did you? If we're going to play the numbers, we need to keep the plant-fertilize-harvest cycle going.

Let me share with you a couple of approaches.

Seed Planting Times 600

Kindra got her business started with 600 e-mails. She decided that her message about storytelling to build your business was a good fit for the American Marketing Association (AMA) audiences. Her plan was to send 600 e-mails to members of the AMA, many of whom worked for Fortune 100 and 500 companies. She thought it would launch her speaking business.

She delivered dozens of presentations booked because of those 600 e-mails. And it did launch her business? Once all of those speeches were delivered, she needed to rinse and repeat. And the cycle began again. Fast forward several years later, Kindra has systems and processes in place to ensure that her funnel stays full.

Her initial seed planting has paid off handsomely and she now has a roster of Fortune 100 clients that many speakers would kill for!

Kindra has taken a very direct approach to her business and has developed systems to sustain it. Here's another example of selling direct.

SUCCESS STORY

David Avrin

Consistency Rules!

We talked earlier about my friend David and his system for getting booked (Strategy #3, Systems). He and his team are planting seeds and following up three to four days of each week.

He has a very strategic and consistent approach. First they identify their market and build a list. Then, his business manager Tiffany starts to connect with each decision-maker through a series of e-mails. Once they get clients on the phone, they close a solid percentage of that business, because Tiffany is terrific.

David goes out to deliver the speech, they work leads from each presentation, rinse and repeat. It's a seed planting numbers game. The more seeds they plant, the more speeches he delivers; the more speeches he delivers, the more spin off is generated.

So when it comes to targeted sales, let's be intentional about how we are going to keep the funnel full (see Exercise 16). Will we choose to be more passive about our approach or direct? And don't get me wrong, just because we called it "passive" doesn't mean there is not work involved. But we're working in batches and streamlining our efforts for the best results.

Exercise 16:

BOOKING BUSINESS

We've discussed two approaches for bringing in the business – passive outbound marketing and selling direct. But which approach will help you to scale your business? Here are some questions to help you decide on your approach.

1. What are you doing currently to keep your funnel full?

____

____

____

2. Is your approach passive outbound, targeted sales or a combination of both?

____

____

____

3. What needs to happen in order to improve the consistency of your funnel?

____

____

____

Going half-baked on any marketing or sales initiative may bring you short-term results but nothing sustainable, and we want to scale!

Consistency Brings Results

No matter which approach you take in keeping your funnel full, the key to it all working will be consistency.

The Wealthy Speaker podcast was around for several years before we finally committed to putting out a weekly show. And it wasn't until we made that promise to ourselves that we saw traction. Once we got serious, each week our numbers grew. And then we hit our stride, and started to see everything change.

That's why overnight success is such a joke. Typically what went into overnight success were years and years of consistent hard work.

Strategy #9

Partnering with Agents, Sponsors & Bureaus

One of your keys to scaling may be to find someone else to help sell you. It's wonderful to imagine that someone like an agency or business manager could manage some or all of your sales. But that's not the only option. There are partners and intermediaries who can also assist in the promoting of your services.

I've worked in two of these roles. Both as a business manager for speakers (remember my story from Strategy #1?) and as the VP of a Speakers Bureau's exclusive division. So I can come at this from a couple of different angles for you.

Let's break down your options.

- Business Managers
- Agents
- Speakers Bureaus
- Sponsors
- Association Partners
- Production/Destination Management Companies

There may very well be other partnerships that you can find – perhaps one of your clients wants to partner with you on a train the trainer program or an app. We'll help you decide which of these avenues are a good fit later, in Exercise 17. Don't limit yourself with the possibilities!

Business Managers

Having someone sell your services is many a business owner's dream come true. It's a team addition that many of us have thought about but it's also one of the trickiest hires. Perhaps because a business manager isn't a position that you want to "scrimp" on. You want to pay this person well so that you get someone who's qualified, someone who rocks at sales.

That's not to say that you can't find a diamond in the rough and groom them into being a superstar. When my first boss (leadership expert Betska K-Burr) rolled the dice on me, I was still a giant lump of coal. She took a chance on me, showed me the ropes, spent the time to build my expertise and confidence and it paid off with her doubling her revenue each year. And that lump of coal turned into a pretty awesome diamond – a sales and marketing expert – me!

Once you have systems and processes for those sales to happen, perhaps hiring a business manager is the way to go. Just remember what we talked about in Strategy #5, on hiring – you want to hire to support the solution as opposed to solving the problem. Betska already knew what it took to sell speeches; she showed me how to do it and I worked within a system that she had already created. She didn't hire me to solve the problem of how to book speeches. She figured it out and then hired me. See the difference?

A business manager could be a position that works from your office, or virtually; that decision will be up to you. Their role in your company should be all about building the business, making sales and growing your bottom line. That could include managing paid ads, outbound marketing, direct selling and everything you read about in Strategy #8, on keeping the funnel full. Be careful when putting administrative duties ($20/hour jobs) on their list or you might not be making the best use of their time.

In the Success Story that follows, we'll talk more about how to put the right people in the right places. In the meantime, be thinking about what traits you want to be looking for in a business manager, and you can document that in the Though-Provoking Questions below. We'll help you decide which of these avenues are a good fit later in Exercise 17.

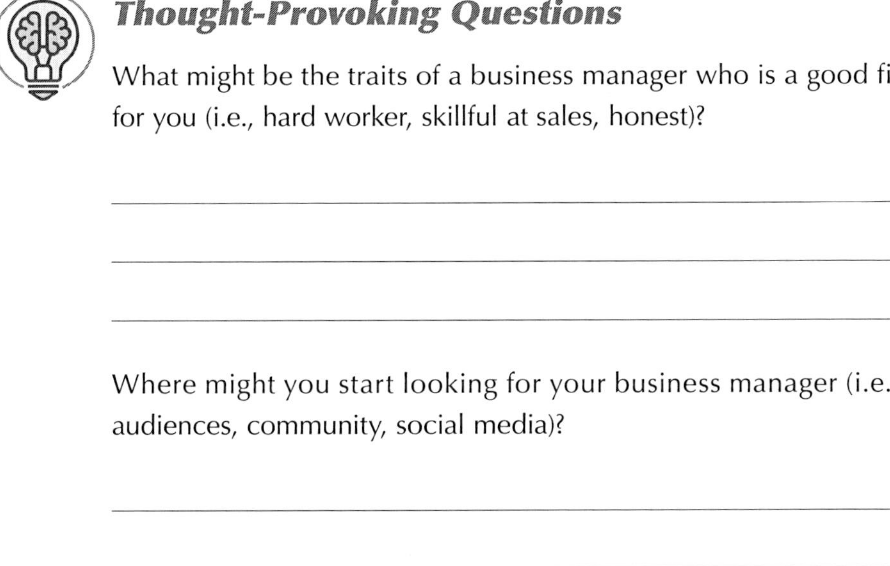

Thought-Provoking Questions

What might be the traits of a business manager who is a good fit for you (i.e., hard worker, skillful at sales, honest)?

____

____

____

Where might you start looking for your business manager (i.e., audiences, community, social media)?

____

____

____

SUCCESS STORY
Jane Atkinson

The Right People in the Right Roles

Several years ago, I finally got smart about how to use my team.

My latest hire (three or four years ago) was the assistant role. And the assistant role pays $25-$35/hour.

Up until the moment of that hire, I was paying up to $50-$70/hour for some of my administrative duties. Why? I didn't have the right team in place, so everything was pretty much going to who I now consider my Content Team.

My Content Team is responsible for my website, my CRM (Customer Relationship Management), blog postings and social media. There's technology involved, and sometimes the hourly rate can go as high as $70. I'm okay with spending that rate on a specialty task.

My website for instance. I know I could have someone change the content on the site for much less, but guess what? I want the best people doing the work on what my customers and prospects see first. My website is not where I'm going to shave the budget. If you've found someone inexpensive who delivers quality, well done. But I've seen speakers who want to charge $10,000 per speech building their own websites to save money. That's a big mistake – unless you're a website designer. This is your prospect's first impression; you cannot sacrifice or cut corners on quality.

I also have a Tech Team for our School – the membership, the course and all of the lessons. I had been assigning some of the customer service elements of the School to them, again, at $70/hour. That rate was too high for those tasks.

My assistant took over those "to do" list items as well, cutting my hourly costs in half. After doing an audit of all of the tasks I had to assign, I was able to reduce my payroll expenses by 40% simply by putting an administrative person in the "catch all" position. Now everything ranging from a customer inquiry to a database change to a scheduling issue gets routed to my assistant at the right hourly rate.

The minute I started delegating the right tasks to the right people, my profits got better and I was in a better position to scale. And my team members were no longer doing jobs that they had no business doing. Putting everyone in their positions based on what they love, and their strengths, made for a much happier team as well.

Agents

An agent is someone who typically works for themselves. It's quite common for agents to work with more than one speaker. Speaker management companies are also agents.

Since the majority of you reading this book are already successful, just looking to ratchet it up a notch or two, an agent may be a good fit. Why? Because most agents aren't looking for people to launch. They want people who are going to make their phone ring. Then, when the phone rings, if they aren't able to book Speaker A for that client, they have a few more in their stable they can turn to.

An agent may ask you to be exclusive with them, meaning that any work that comes into your funnel gets handed to them. They likely get paid a monthly fee plus commission. So you'll want to be in a position where paying this fee won't break the bank.

Whether you hire a business manager or an agent, you want them to feel success early in your relationship. One booked speaking engagement can fuel the fire and make them want to work harder. Try to support that idea by handing them a few "cherries" or business that is really close to being closed.

You also want to make sure that you spend a lot of time on the front end feeding them "product knowledge." The more they have seen you speak (preferably live) and have been on sales calls with you, the better this will go.

Because they work on commission, when you win agents and speakers bureaus win too. So help them help you!

What you don't want is for six months to go by and they haven't made a sale. You'll start to feel resentful over the money being spent each month. Work hard to get them up and running and selling quickly. All of these same tips apply to hiring a Business Manager or anyone in the sales role for your company.

Speakers Bureaus

By now you likely know that there are two ways of working with speakers bureaus – exclusive and non-exclusive. (For a deeper dive on when to start working with bureaus, refer to *The Wealthy Speaker 2.0*, Chapter 6.)

Exclusive with a Bureau

The bureau business has taken its share of hits over the years. Working off a 25% commission (which then is split between the bureau agent and the bureau owner), many bureaus have realized that it's not easy to make a living with this model. Around the time that I worked for the bureau in Dallas, we realized that having an *exclusive* speakers division could help change all that. The exclusive arrangement means that you (the speaker) send all of your inquiries to the bureau. Even if another bureau wants to book you, they have to co-broker with your exclusive bureau, thus making the phone ring for them.

It's a good idea and many speakers bureaus are taking on exclusive speakers. This is where trust and communication become even more important because you have to trust that a bureau is going to do a great job of following up every lead that you hand them. And, like everything else, there are some folks who will do it amazingly well and some that will drop the ball.

You should note that if you work with several bureaus already, you need to be prepared for the bureaus you do not go exclusive with to drop off in business. Splitting a commission is one reason, but putting your client details into the hands of another bureau (a competitor) is hard for some people. It takes a ton of trust. Unless the demand for you is huge, you may see a drop in your bureau business once you go exclusive. If the bureau you choose sends you a ton of business directly, this will be a non-issue.

Thought-Provoking Questions

Is there a bureau booking who gives you plenty of business now? Enough to sustain you?

___

___

___

Which bureaus have the best relationships with other bureaus (co-brokering)?

___

___

___

Non-Exclusive Bureau Work

The non-exclusive agreement with a bureau is more of a no brainer. It's true you have to give up 25% commission on each piece of business, but that was business you didn't have in the first place. When someone else calls you and says, "Hey, I have a client who'd like to book you," well, it's icing on the cake of your business model.

Some speakers have 30% of their business come from bureaus, some 50% and some even more than that. Many have a dozen different bureaus working on their behalf and that's pretty darn cool and works on a beautiful principal called "leverage."

Typically the issues at this level become more about managing your calendar, and multiple holds, sometimes for the same engagement from different bureaus. When you are the "flavor of the month" as a speaker, many bureaus may submit you for the same job, which creates drama. (My philosophy on this, BTW, is that the business goes to whoever the client chooses to work with for that booking.)

I'd hesitate before encouraging you to let more than 50% of your calendar go out to booking partners. Staying in touch with clients via direct bookings allows you to keep a bit more control of your calendar and you're not then putting all of your eggs in one basket.

An additional reason for watching your bureau/direct bookings ratio reared its head when COVID hit in early 2020. When you have 100% of your business with speakers bureaus, and all of the engagements get postponed or canceled, you haven't collected any deposits at that point. Nor do you have any control over negotiating with the client and potentially upselling a package that includes virtual events right away plus live events in the future. The control is in someone else's hands.

You'll likely want to be partnering with speakers bureaus in most any scenario. Having people who understand how to sell you and having access to a huge customer database is a lovely bonus. And if you are too frugal to pay the 25% and see the value of leveraging your time in this way, then I'll assume that you already have all of the business you can handle.

Sponsors

Imagine a big bank comes to you and says, "Our small business customers need to hear your message."

"Great!" You say, "I'm game!" And they want to take you on a cross-country tour to share your presentation to thousands of their customers in 20 different cities. How cool is that?

Well, it's happened before and it's likely to happen again. Joe Calloway was invited to speak to Chase Bank's customers in 24 cities over two months. A brilliant experience for Joe and the bank.

Imagine a big mutual fund company loves your message and wants to use you as a spokesperson for their fund. Or a pharmaceutical company wants to put you in front of all of their doctors. You're not necessarily pushing their drug, you're pushing your message and they are the sponsor of said message.

A large bank recognizes that female business owners are a growing part of their market. They hire you, an expert on Entrepreneurial Women, to travel around the country to speak to groups of their customers on growing their businesses.

When you align yourself with corporate sponsors, it allows you to get your message out there (possibly prompting more spin off) and creates the goodwill that the corporation wants with their end users. Maybe you teach customer service in such a way that a big technology company wants you to do a series of events for their users.

Or maybe a company loves your work and because you both target real estate, they agree to step in and sponsor your event whenever the realtor client doesn't have the budget?

The goal with any sponsorship agreement is to come with a win-win. And I don't know that any two sponsorships are created equally.

Pretty much everything is up for potential sponsorship. A good example? Look at social media influencers who sponsor things like designer clothes. You wear my clothes, post it to your millions of followers and I'll pay you for that. Speakers have not typically gone that far down the sponsorship path, but the possibilities are definitely there. If you love your Chucks (Chuck Taylor sneakers) and you talk about them from the stage, there may be a sponsorship opportunity for you.

When negotiating a sponsorship or the terms of a multi-engagement deal, the natural response might be to negotiate downward on the fee. But I'd encourage you to put a package together, based on reaching the desired goal for the company and throw extra value in to make it more exclusive (thus expensive) per engagement. We'll talk more about sponsorship packages shortly, but here's a story about not giving away the farm.

Getting Paid What You're Worth

My friend and former client, Greg, offers leadership training for frontline workers in the manufacturing sector. He steps outside this sector on occasion, but this is his primary focus. He puts together huge (sometimes seven-figure) training contracts with sometimes 50 training days for one company.

Not exactly a sponsorship arrangement, but the point is Greg recommends that we don't lower the fee for multiple engagements because it's often more work, not less.

One of the benefits of "picking a lane" is that you become known for one thing. For Greg, it's helping frontline leaders grow their skills and lead to better outcomes. So when he and the client first start talking, the client has likely already recognized that they have a need for this type of training and is starting to shop around. It's not Greg's goal to be the lowest price.

When he puts together a proposal, it's not for one speech; it's often for a year-long, multi-city agreement designed to create a stronger leadership culture at the frontline level. The deliverables might include: workshops in leadership, communication, motivation and conflict, combined with a tool for tracking how participants are applying what they learn and how it is impacting their department.

And for big outcomes like this, the clients are ready and willing to spend the big bucks.

I tell you Greg's story because it might inspire you to revisit how you price things. You may not have any interest in "training" like this per se, but there might be something that catches your eye. And when it comes to sponsorships, I don't want you to sell yourself short.

Sponsorship Packages

If you design a sponsorship package, please know that it may be a long sale and it's going to be a ton of work! So make sure you price it accordingly.

Multiple engagement bookings can offer lots of benefits to you and your client, but it can also be a great deal of work. Be careful not to sell yourself short!

Think about what all you can include in a package that might sweeten the pot? Perhaps they purchase books for the entire audience in each city. Perhaps there is a follow-up video series or smaller group Zoom meetings after the event. Maybe you include live VIP gatherings. All of these features point towards adding value to the client and getting to the desired outcome.

Thought-Provoking Questions

Who could you be building better long-term relationships with?

____

____

____

What kind of sponsorship opportunities might you keep your eyes peeled for?

____

____

____

How might you add value so that you can get paid what you're worth?

____

____

____

Association Partners

You are an expert in the leadership space with a niche in retail, and the national association of retail leaders comes to you with an idea to pilot a new program. Yahoo! When anyone else can put bums in seats and sell a program for you, that's a bonus!

I had the National Speakers Association, Michigan Chapter, approach me about doing a pilot program for their Chapter using The Wealthy Speaker School as the content for the program. One of the board members came to me and said, "I was at a meeting last week with our President to talk about our Speakers Academy (that's a program they offer for new speakers to help them jump-start their business) and we wondered if you might want to partner with us so that we don't have to reinvent the wheel?"

I was thrilled that they had asked me to partner with them and do hope that it all goes smoothly when we test the program. It could potentially mean that we get dozens of people through our School every year that we might not have secured otherwise. And perhaps more Chapters will hop on the bandwagon. (I've been around this association for several decades and I know politics may play a part in this, so I'm not counting my chickens just yet.)

Who might you partner with to see your programs move into bigger markets? When you lock into deals with groups like this, remember not to give the farm away, but also that it's business that you might not have otherwise. This approach is especially important if you can deliver your part of the agreement without any input or work from you (like my deal with the NSA Michigan group).

One of my past clients, Steve Little, took advantage of this idea years ago to do a Chamber of Commerce tour. Steve designed a presentation specifically for Chamber members, shared with the Board how to sell it to their members, gave them a special flat rate and toured the country for a year with his message for small- and mid-sized businesses.

Production/Destination Management Companies

As I've mentioned, one of my best buds in this industry is Kris Young and she's worked for years for speakers bureaus and production companies. In her role, she secured both speakers and entertainment. And let me tell you, she worked with companies with incredibly deep pockets.

The next time you are at a speaking engagement where a production company has been hired, make sure that you tap into the people in the back of the room running the show. Not only do they have your current performance in the palm of their hands – they can make you look very, very good if they want to – they could also be a resource for you for future business.

And sidebar, if they are filming, you can offer them a little incentive (like an Amazon gift card) to shoot you a copy of the recording lickety-split. It's much harder for them to blow off sending you the video with that gift card burning a hole in their pocket.

Production companies may be a path to more business. After all, they have a lot of great clients and in some cases, like Kris's company, they offer up suggestions for speakers and entertainment to provide the full conference service to their clients.

Destination Management Companies

Although I hear of this less in our world, business can also come from a destination management company. They are often one of the first hires for an event. Their primary service is to help the client find a city and venue to bring their group to. But guess what? They could also recommend speakers.

Some destination companies keep a database of local talent in each city so that they can offer more service to their clients. And, it wouldn't be a stretch that they might request a finder's fee from the speakers who they refer.

There are a lot of working parts that go into a large national meeting. At any given point during a gathering of the meeting organizers, your name could be put forward! And the goal is not that you book these one at a time, but that you have a steady flow of industry partner leads coming to you so that you are able to work less and earn more.

• • •

Now that we've explored the various partnerships that may be formed, run through Exercise 17 to see what is right for you.

Exercise 17:

WHO IS THE RIGHT PARTNER FOR YOU?

Creating partnerships and scaling your business go hand in hand. Some relationships may seem obvious to manage your sales, but there are other collaborations that are definite winners. This chapter discussed a lot of the options, but here you can review each one, decide what might be the best fit and write down your first action items.

Business Manager

A business manager might be a good fit for you if:

1. You can't handle the influx of business that is coming into your office (you don't have time to follow up leads) or
2. You can easily afford to pay someone to generate new business using a system you already have in place.

____

____

____

Agent

An agent might be a good fit for you if:

1. You don't have time to follow up all of the business that is coming in your door or
2. You can easily afford to pay someone to generate new business for you.

____

____

____

Speakers Bureaus

An exclusive arrangement might be a good fit if:

1. You have gotten a ton of business with the bureau in question and really like working with them or
2. You don't want to manage the day-to-day work associated with the leads coming into your business or
3. You have other sources of income.

____

____

____

Sponsorships

When thinking about who you might partner with for sponsorships consider these ideas.

1. Who wants to get in front of the same audiences that you do?

____

____

____

2. Who also has customers/clients in the space that you work in? (Check trade show sponsors in the industry events that you attend as a starting point.)

____

____

____

Associations

Building relationships with associations can take some work.

1. Is there an association that you might partner with to widen your reach?

____

____

____

2. How can you create and present this option to associations that have already hired you?

____

____

____

Production/Destination Management Companies

1. Are there destination management companies you have worked with in the past?

____

____

____

2. Which companies are located in your backyard (closest major city)?

____

____

____

Strategy #10

You Know How to Make Money, How Do You Keep It?

Something essential for scaling your business is cash flow. If you are always robbing Peter to pay Paul, it's going to be very difficult to scale.

Since you are reading this book, I'm assuming that you already know how to make money, and a lot of it. Probably a lot more than the average bear makes in a year, am I right? But a few of you, not all, might need help and inspiration to figure out how to better "keep" more of that money. And, I'd also like to talk a bit about your mindset when it comes to money.

How Do You Feel About Money?

Examining our thoughts and feelings about money isn't something we always stop to think about. But it's worthy of reflection.

What were you taught about money growing up?

- Money doesn't grow on trees (that's mine).
- Money is the root of all evil.
- People with money are mean.
- You have to work your fingers to the bone to make a lot of money.
- You can't be spiritual and have money.

When we really stop and scrutinize how we were raised and what our current beliefs are about money, it can be liberating.

Taking time now to uncover any subconscious roadblocks that you have to money is essential for growth.

The Money Thermostat

I heard the term "money thermostat" from Stu McLaren. My money thermostat used to be set at about $75K. I'd make that much in a year and when I started to see myself creeping up towards $150, somehow (through sabotage or whatever means) I was always finding myself right back at $75K.

This became very clear when I worked as a business manager for the publisher Peter Legge. I had moved from a basement office and straight commission (money struggle) to a corner office and big salary. But my money mindset had not caught up. I worked my butt off. Out of a company of over 100 people, I was often the last one to leave at night. But on some level, I didn't think I deserved to make so much money. So what did I do? I sabotaged the situation. I left that job to start over at zero salary in Dallas. Peter and I are still friends and laugh about this now, but I just wasn't ready to earn so much money.

What made the difference, and the breakthrough once and for all, was doing the money work inside my brain. Whereas before, I didn't think I deserved to make that much, now I see the sky as the limit. Whereas before I thought you had to bust your butt in order to earn over a million per year, now I see that with systems and processes in place, in can be done while keeping my exact same work schedule.

And as for problems? You'll have the similar problems at $100K, as you have at $500K and at a million. No business is without problems. Where there are people, there are problems. Where there is money, there are problems. Staying on top of your taxes, for instance, is a problem that just keeps getting bigger. But why not check out the seven-figure problems and try them on for size? I'll bet you don't find that they are all that different.

Some people worry that if they make too much money their friends and family won't like them anymore. Well, guess what? It doesn't have to be public knowledge. Go about your business and keep your numbers to yourself. It's nobody's business how much money you make. Perhaps your kids will be pleasantly surprised when they learn from reading your will that they had "the millionaire next door" as their parent.

I'm certainly not that subtle. I'd love nothing more than to be able to take our entire family, two adult daughters and husbands, and six grandkids on a special vacation every year. Maybe we start out with cruises and work our way towards – the big dream – a hop on, hop off, round the world private jet tour. Imagine being able to give your kids that experience? To expose them to things they'd never do on their own? Part of what drives me is wanting to do nice things for our family. That's my "why."

Thought-Provoking Question

Have you ever found that you had a money thermostat?

____

____

____

Revisit Your Why

We've heard Simon Sinek talking about starting with "why." Why is that you do the work you do? What drives that?

Many of you have service at the top of your list and I think that is beautiful and noble. Perhaps there's a bit more to it as well? You want to help people *and* you want to sail around the world with your partner on a decadent yacht. There is nothing wrong with wanting to live whatever *your* version of The Wealthy Speaker Lifestyle is.

And as we talked about in the "How Do You Feel About Money" section above, if you feel that you can't align your wealthy speaker goals with your spiritual beliefs, you've got some work to do. There is absolutely nothing wrong with living where you want to live, driving whatever car you want, sailing away on your yacht or beyond!

There's nothing I love more than showing people what's possible in their lives. Sometimes when you are living in the thick of the day to day, it's hard to see your way out to a better path. But when you're the coach, looking in from the outside, the sky is the limit.

That's what my coaches have done for me. When I was a single woman living in Dallas, it was a stretch to imagine myself married and with little kids running around at my lake house in Canada. But that's what I imagined. It was this beautiful life. I really don't even know how I dreamed it up, but I know I made it happen. By using all of the steps in this book combined with the power of an unstoppable mind.

If it's other people you're worried about, remember the person who's probably judging your desires the most is you. Get over it! "Oh, what will people think if I purchase this new Tesla?" They'll think, "That's a damn nice car. I wish I had one!" And when they say "must be nice," you can honestly say, "Thank you, it is." You know how hard you worked to get the lifestyle that you desire!

Don't try to make others feel better about themselves by playing small. Be an example of what's possible!

Taking the kids on vacation is one "why" but a few years ago, I discovered a bigger one.

I've been saying for quite some time that I want my husband to retire so that we can be mobile. I can see him working part time at a golf course in lieu of memberships for us. (Notice how I worked myself in on that deal!) When he gets home in the early afternoon each day, I'm done work and we can go have fun.

In the summers we'll live at our cottage up north (in Ontario, near Tobermory for those of you who know it) and somewhere south in the winters, maybe Florida. I've thought about having a retreat center and bringing people to me during the winters.

That's my "why" big picture but let me give you one more layer.

When my husband was 45, he had a heart attack. He's now 63 and there's been no signs of heart problems whatsoever. But keeping him alive is my primary goal so that we can live out this dream together. And if that means that he gives up his business a bit earlier than planned, then I'm game. I don't have him convinced quite yet, he really loves his work, but we are slowly taking steps in that direction.

So, what's your why for scaling your business? Use Exercise 18 to explore this question.

Exercise 18: WHAT'S YOUR WHY?

Scaling your business is a big undertaking – it's taken a whole book to reveal the strategies – so you want to be clear on your why. Take a look back at Your Perfect Day and Scaling Checklist (Exercises 1 and 2) and consider this question.

Why do you want to scale your business?

____

____

____

____

____

____

____

____

____

Your Income – Love It or Leave It

Let's circle back to Brooke Castillo's Thought Model that I shared with you in Strategy #1. When you earn income, if you have negative feelings attached to that earning, they may impede your ability to earn more. Now I know that sounds "out there," but if any of the revenue that you earn has a stigma attached to it there may be trouble.

Here are some examples I've heard.

- I feel like a sell-out because I only took the job for the money.
- I hate delivering this product or that service.
- I really don't like working with this client.
- The idea of developing and selling the service feels like moving a giant boulder up a steep hill.

If any of these sound like a situation in your business, you might want to consider letting it go. And we covered how to Subtract in Order to Add in Strategy #4.

There is another option. The alternative is to embrace that money. It's a love or leave it decision. My client Frank had to make this decision.

SUCCESS STORY

Frank Somma

Loving Every Dollar

I talked to my mastermind client Frank about his side hustle of selling photocopiers. A sales expert, Frank had put together a very lucrative business model that allowed him to spend a few hours each day selling copiers to his favorite clients, and left him open to building his speaking business for the bulk of his day.

When we examined how Frank felt about that copier business, we realized he needed a slight shift in his thinking. His old thought was, "I never intended to be selling copiers at 62 years of age. That wasn't the plan." That thought put some negative feelings around that very healthy monthly income. A friend of Frank's, from the copier business, helped him recognize that he had intentionally built this plan for himself, and had asked to keep only the best copier clients on his list.

All he had to do was appreciate the income!

Once the shift was to more of a place of gratitude for those clients, Frank started appreciating all of the income he received. And funny enough, he started to see more revenue flowing in from all of the areas of his business.

What income are you bringing in that you have negative feelings about?

You have two choices. Subtract it or appreciate it. The goal is to be intentional no matter which one you choose.

Thought-Provoking Question

Is this income that needs to be subtracted in order to grow? Or, do I simply need to make peace with it and have gratitude for that income?

____

____

____

Make Nice with Your Money, or You Won't Get More

You have two choices. You can appreciate all of the income that you bring in, like Frank did, or you can let it go.

There's something to be said for security and I suspect that when the time is right, and your income from your day job (like Frank's) is being replaced by your speaking income, you'll know it.

Let's talk about fear for a second. I think that the majority of the reason we hang on to clients who are no longer serving us is related to fear – fear that there won't be another client. It's well known that every actor's worst nightmare is that they will never get another part. It's hard to let that go no matter how much stardom you've achieved.

Make decisions about what to let go of from a place of confidence, not fear.

Years ago, my boss Peter Legge, a multimillionaire, told me that "decisions based in fear are typically wrong." This idea stuck with me throughout the years and I've shared it with thousands of speakers.

So the question becomes, "If you are 100% clear on the value that you offer, will that not eliminate that fear? If you are 100% confident that you will achieve your goals, does that not quiet the voice of doubt?"

But, when an economic disaster hits, all of the fear rises up to the surface. And guess what? It has the ability to set you back. Then I think back to Meridith's story (remember her, in Strategy #1, running towards the fire, with the hose?), and I realize that it's a choice whether or not fear gets to play a role in your business, even in the most challenging times. You will find a way to serve your clients and earn what you are worth by having fear take a backseat to good old-fashioned, roll-up-your-sleeves hard work. And do we have to work 60 hours a week during difficult times? I think not.

Holding Your Boundaries in Rough Times

I think you should stand firmly in the boundaries you've set for yourself when it comes to fees, your schedule, and working with clients you don't love.

My schedule has typically been to record podcasts on Mondays (taking the summer off), coach on Tuesday through Thursday and take Friday's off. Did I still take every Friday off mid-pandemic? Yep! It didn't occur to me not to. Did I take a week's vacation every month that summer despite the economy? You bet! My friend Rhonda told me about this idea a few years ago. Every time there's a holiday Monday, my husband and I take the rest of the week off.

My work day is typically done by three in the afternoon. That's when my mental capacity starts to wind down. Did I turn down exciting work that was outside of my parameters? Yep, I did. When a great opportunity came from overseas, but the conference required me to speak at 11 PM or 6 AM my time, I knew I wouldn't do my best work, and passed on it.

The 2020 pandemic could have easily been a year when fear drove the bus. A time when I didn't take vacation, when I worked on my scheduled days off, when I accepted business to speak at ungodly hours of the day.

But my boundaries held.

And when a past client who wasn't a very nice person, circled back to ask to re-join our School, although the revenue would have been nice, we said, "Thank you, but it's not a good fit." We've turned away a few people and not taking "wrong fit" clients feels good.

Getting – and keeping (still to come in this strategy) – money is something that we want to be more intentional about. Be aware of when you are stepping outside of your boundaries and regretting taking on business. Don't let fear drive the bus.

Your Comfort Fund

When we accept business that doesn't bring us joy, we pay the price.

Have you ever gotten to tax season, looked at your very healthy income and thought, "Now, where the heck did all that money go?"

A couple of years ago in one of my Strategic Coach® sessions, our instructor, Teresa, talked about putting together a "reserve fund." You can call it what you want – comfort fund, rainy day fund, mad money fund, emergency stash – whatever you like. The point is that Teresa really got me thinking about a fund that would allow you to *not* worry about money. Here's her story.

SUCCESS STORY Teresa Esler

Building Your Reserve Fund

Teresa, communication coach and business strategist, has also served as my coach/instructor at Strategic Coach® for the past five years. She's someone who I admire, and when she talks about her own business, I get a ton of great ideas.

During a session a few years ago, Teresa talked about never having to worry about money again. "Hmmmm," I wondered. "What's that feel like?" This whole concept of worrying about money felt like it was stitched into my DNA. But Teresa started me down a different thought path.

Teresa told us about her Reserve Fund. She explained that she had put a sizable amount into this fund so that no matter what happened in her life, her business and in the world, she would be okay. She wouldn't worry about money.

Well, not long later, Teresa's resolve was tested. Shannon, her assistant of 20 years and also one of her best friends, announced she had cancer. A devastating blow, both personally and for Teresa's business as Shannon played a major role in her company's success.

At the same time, Teresa's mom was fighting dementia and lived several hours away. She took time away from the business to care for her mom.

Not much time passed before all of Teresa's speaking engagements went away with the COVID pandemic, a third strike, testing her resilience to the core.

But through it all, Teresa's Reserve Fund allowed her to focus on family, her sick friend and not worry when income simply vanished due to a global virus. Her Reserve put her in a position to roll through changes without losing her sense of well-being or stressing out completely over money.

The Reserve Fund saved the day.

After hearing Teresa's story, I set about putting some cash aside for my Comfort Fund. That's what I call it, because it makes me feel a little bit more comfortable. (Exercise 19 will help you set up yours.) It wasn't a ton of money, but I have to tell you that in a time of crisis, just seeing that money sitting there in the account made me feel so much better. There's a huge psychological advantage to not worrying about money day in, day out and that's helping to rewire my DNA to not worry about money.

Exercise 19: COMFORT FUND

1. What amount in your comfort fund (or emergency stash or rainy day or mad money fund) makes you feel like you never have to worry about money?

   ____

   ____

   ____

2. By when do you want to have your comfort fund in place (if it's not already in place)?

   ____

   ____

   ____

Investing Outside of the Business

Okay, so let's imagine that you have your comfort fund in place. What might you do to diversify your portfolio? Now, I know I'm likely kicking at an open door here, but for those of you who haven't thought about it, how can you expand into other areas?

My husband and I have real estate going for us. We'll cash out of at least two (of four) properties at some point and have a nice retirement on top of our investments. I could try to set up my business to sell, and I haven't ruled that out. Having systems to bring business in the door in droves is the key to that working and I'm not there yet. (I'm working on it!)

Joe Calloway has dabbled in investments outside of the speaking business many times over the years. He was once a restaurant owner, has invested in several start-ups, including a snowboard company (pretty cool!), and is also an investor with a real estate conglomerate that buys apartment buildings. That's a 30-year speaking business and quite a bit to show for it!

How are you rounding out your portfolio by stepping outside of your business?

- Real estate
- Stocks, RSPs, 401Ks
- Start-ups
- House flipping
- Other investments

Remember the goal here is not just to make money, but to also keep it. If you have your comfort fund and retirement portfolio in great shape then maybe you start to look at some of these on the list.

Many of us know how to make a lot of money, but learning how to keep money is something that (if you aren't great at it) you want to move more into the forefront in your mind. Being intentional with "keeping money" holds a lot of power.

Final Thoughts

Well, we've talked through all of the ten Strategies for Scaling. I hope you have a long list of ideas to implement as a result. Here are a few final thoughts.

Are We Having Fun Yet?

Remember to reward yourself for hard work. I think that a lot of us forget to celebrate the victories along the way.

What's something memorable that you can give yourself when you've achieved a goal? Maybe it's a resort weekend or a new hot tub when you've hit a money milestone. Remembering to stop and celebrate – even the smallest things – is really imperative. Don't let those important moments pass you by!

On a daily basis, we need to take time to acknowledge what's been accomplished. Counting every single win leads to momentum. One of my favorite apps is called "Win Streak" (also by Dan Sullivan). Every day at 4 PM my phone or iPad pings me and asks me, "What were your wins today?"

There are days when I initially think there is nothing to report, but once you get into the swing of Win Streak, you're surprised at how the small things add up. When you write down "went for a walk" that might not seem like that much but guess what? When you string together walks five days in a row, it adds up to better health and well-being. Some of my clients are so hard on themselves. They'll work around the clock and will acknowledge none of it. Be sure to recognize all of the wins you have achieved, no matter how big or small.

Being an entrepreneur is about building the life and the business of your dreams. Are you remembering to enjoy the journey? Although 2020 was a rough year, it brought many speakers off the road and allowed them to take inventory of what they loved and didn't love about this business. Be sure to check in and make sure that you are loving every piece of your business.

Life is too short to do work that you loathe!

Can You Really Make This Happen?

Is it possible to work less while making more?

I'm here to tell you that's a big old "Heck yeah!" What you're going to be doing is getting more intentional about how you work. You're going to start asking yourself, "Should I really be doing this?" You're going to be putting the team members in place to take over those $20 and $30 per hour jobs.

If you start to doubt your path to scaling your business, if you ever start to feel overwhelmed with how much there is to do, I want you to remember that you only have to take one step at a time. One client at a time. One hire at a time. One Standard Operating Procedure at a time.

Being impatient about your journey is not the way to go when it comes to scaling.

Believe me, I'm living this approach first hand. I have a goal to get to $1.7 million and I'm not as close as I'd like to be. But I've really relaxed into the journey. I'm enjoying the lessons that I've gotten during my path to scaling. Heck, I've learned some great lessons just writing this book!

I've made lots of mistakes, which have set me back, but they were critical to becoming the leader that I needed to be in order to get here. There's a chance I won't get to my goal, but when I think about that, I remind myself that I've pretty much nailed every goal I've ever set out for myself. I have proven over and over that I can do anything I put my mind to. Is getting way past a million easy? Well, maybe not, but it's all just steps and strategy, and I've done steps and strategy before. So I don't sweat it too much. And my belief in myself is 100% of the equation.

So do you believe that you can scale?

If you take your time and set the stage for what's to come, if you put your systems and your team in place, if you map out your offerings based on what you love and drop things that aren't serving you, if you partner up with some good people and turn up the volume on the things that are working, and if you're ready to double down on your success, then I believe you can do this!!!

Chances are you've already had a level of success and now we're just multiplying that. You can do this, you have the talent, the expertise, the skill and the know how to get 'er done!

Dreaming Big

We started out *Scaling Your Speaking Business* by talking about not limiting yourself in your dreams. I've watch as my mentors Dan and Brooke built businesses up to the tens, and potentially hundreds, of millions of dollars. I've helped thousands of my clients move into healthy six-figure businesses, and several more again to high six- and seven-figure businesses. I know it can be done!

And, it can be done without killing yourself to get there. My dad was an engineer, who earned $60,000 a year. That seemed like a fortune at the time. When I experienced my first $60,000 month, he just shook his head and laughed. "And you're still taking every Friday off?" he'd ask. "Yep, sure do," I said. I sure miss his laughing, and how often he told me he was proud of me.

My parents' generation taught us "money doesn't grow on trees." They couldn't imagine the type of success that we are having, nor could they really understand it. In fact, most people don't understand our business model. So don't try to explain what you are doing to your extended family; they may not get it. My dad just laughed and scratched his head and I love that he never scoffed at my goal to work less and earn more.

I hope that you've been thinking about your dream lifestyle and what that looks like to you. As I wrap up this book, I'm about ten steps from my paddle board. The lake, where I've done the majority of the writing, is as flat as a pancake, not a ripple on it. I can hear a loon calling out, "Come on, Jane, hop on that board!" Ten years ago this cottage and lifestyle was just a pipe dream. But this is my version of "wealthy" and it doesn't include speaking at all.

It seemed so far from reality many years ago, but somewhere along the line, someone planted a seed of possibility in my mind. And it grew and grew until the next thing I knew I was living the exact life of my dreams. I hope I am that seed planter for you.

I know that whatever your vision for your dream life and business looks like, it is possible. Do not put any limits on it. Just take one step at a time, one strategy at a time and keep moving in that direction. Before you know it, you'll be living it!

And I hope that when you get there, you'll drop me a line and let me know how you made out. Will you?

Or, if you need any help sorting through all of your options and ideas, I'm always standing by with our Focus 40 coaching session. Check it out.

I can't wait to hear about your success,

See you soon Wealthy Speaker!

PS: Don't forget to check out your Bonus Page for all the exercises, thought-provoking questions, links and more!

And, if you have been taking action while moving through this book, it might be a good time to revisit Your Scaling Checklist (Exercise 2 from Are You Ready to Scale).

Acknowledgements

Thank you to my amazing book team, Catherine Leek of Green Onion Publishing (my editor and project manager) and Kim Monteforte (my cover and interior designer). We've worked together over a decade and the amount of trust we have in each other is beautiful.

And finally, Team Jane would not be complete without my husband John and our family. You are everything to me. It's been so much fun building this beautiful life together! Our girls Emily (Justin) and Katie (Justin) and our amazing grandchildren Jayden, Hazel, Ella, Zoe, Cooper, and one player to be named later (exciting) are what drive me and this business.